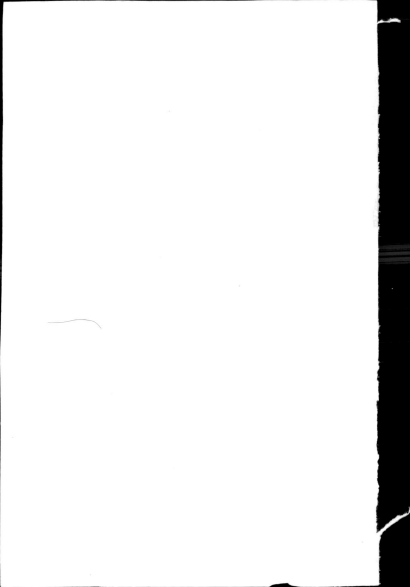

CLIMBERS' GUIDE
TO THE CAIRNGORMS AREA

CLIMBERS' GUIDE TO THE
CAIRNGORMS AREA

BY

MALCOLM SMITH

VOL. I
(NORTHERN DISTRICT)
THE CAIRNGORMS

PUBLISHED BY
THE SCOTTISH MOUNTAINEERING CLUB
369 HIGH STREET, EDINBURGH
1961

FIRST PUBLISHED . . . 1961

PRINTED IN GREAT BRITAIN BY
ROBERT CUNNINGHAM AND SONS LTD, ALVA

ACKNOWLEDGEMENTS

WITHOUT the aid of T. W. Patey, the Editor's constant associate in the venture from 1954 to 1956, this guide could not have been written. His enthusiasm was instrumental in laying its foundations, and from his observations, explorations and original notes much of its material is composed. To him also is the credit for the policy adopted in the classification of summer and winter routes.

The Editor is also greatly indebted to his associates of the Etchachan Club whose support was as inspiring as their information on new climbs was exhausting. In particular he wishes to thank G. H. Leslie and D. E. Scoffin who drew ten and four diagrams respectively. G. H. Leslie prepared the maps.

Other thanks for their valuable assistance are due to the following members of the Club:

W. D. Brooker, for notes on winter routes.

William A. Ewen, whose work on the rock-climbing sections of the S.M.C. Guide *The Cairngorms* was of great importance and was freely drawn upon.

J. Y. L. Hay, who drew three diagrams.

R. H. Sellers, who drew seven diagrams.

J. M. Taylor, for his aid during the exploratory stages of the guide.

Adam Watson Jnr., who seconded on a host of climbs, often in atrocious weather, and took aneroid heights of several cliffs.

CONTENTS

EDITOR'S NOTES

THE S.M.C. Guide *The Cairngorms*, while named after the principal summits in the region it covers, deals fully with other mountain groups covering a large area of North-East Scotland. This climbers' guide, to avoid confusion, and to be complementary to that publication, embraces the climbs in all areas covered by it, viz. The Cairngorms: Lochnagar–Broad Cairn: Glen Clova: Glen Callater: Glen Isla. A single guide to describe all the routes in this vast area would not be of pocketable size and this consideration has made it necessary to produce an edition in two volumes. Volume I (Northern District) comprises the Cairngorms proper, Volume II (Southern District) comprises the Lochnagar–Broad Cairn–Glen Clova region.

As many corries are shared by two or more summits it has been found impossible for the sake of clarity to group the climbs under separate mountains. The layout used may therefore appear unorthodox, but to the Editor seemed to offer the best solution.

While fully appreciating the urge for exploration he has not included (with the exception of Clova) the ultra-short climbs of the 100-foot–120-foot order, the scope for which in the Cairngorms is immense. His reason stems mainly from his view that the cliffs of these great summits should encourage the mountaineer with his route-finding rather than the specialist and his short problems, and also from his opinion that against the long approaches to the corries the short climb offers too little reward. That all may be changed in a future edition is realised, yet while major routes are not in short supply the exclusion is felt to be justified.

A policy of specifying the best and most enjoyable

routes has been adopted. By this it is hoped to foster in climbers from other districts a greater interest in the rock-climbing potentialities of the area.

Finally, the prerequisite of any rock-climbing guide is a consistent assessment of difficulty. With this end in view all the climbs were investigated by the Editor and his associates during the seasons 1954–1958.

KEY TO DIAGRAM No. 1

MAP OF CAIRNGORMS MASSIF

1. Coire Garbhlach
2. Buttresses of Sgòran Dubh Mor and Sgòr Gaoith.
3. Coire an Lochain
4. Coire Ruadh
5. Coire Beanaidh
6. Sròn na Lairig
7. Coire Bhrochain
8. Garbh Choire Dhaidh
9. Garbh Choire Mor
10. Bivouac
11. Devil's Point
12. Corrour Bothy
13. Coire Cath nam Fionn
14. Coire Sputan Dearg
15. Creagan a'Choire Etchachan
16. Hutchison Hut
17. Cairn Etchachan
18. Beinn Mheadhoin
19. Shelter Stone
20. Hell's Lum Crag
21. Stag Rocks
22. Sinclair Hut
23. Creag an Leth-choin (Lurcher's Crag)
24. Coire an Lochain
25. Coire an t-Sneachda
26. Jean's Hut
27. Garbh Choire
28. Coire nan Clach
29. Bivouac
30. Coire an Dubh Lochain
31. Coire na Ciche

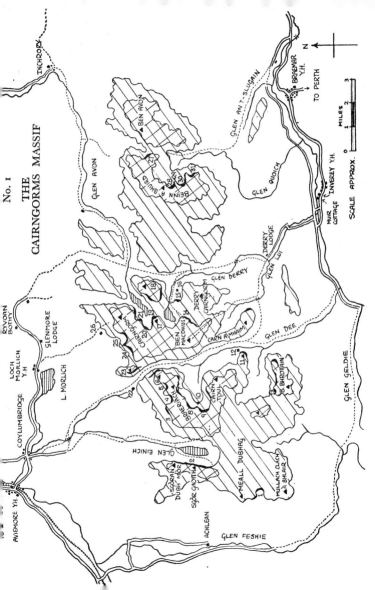

No. I
THE
CAIRNGORMS MASSIF

N

SCALE APPROX.

0   1   2   3
MILES

DIAGRAMS

INTRODUCTION

THE charm which the Cairngorms exert is of a puzzling nature, for they lack the picturesque form of the peaks of Skye and the West Coast. Perhaps the secret lies in their vastness; the limitless plateaux, the great pine-forests of their glens and foothills, the immense scale on which the whole scene is set. Ideally they are mountains to be explored, for one can never know them wholly and every visit brings to light some hitherto unknown feature.

It is not surprising therefore to find them the Mecca of the walker, rather than climber. Consequently the apt, yet unfortunate phrase "the hill-walker's paradise" has been engendered to describe them—unfortunate in its liability to mislead; for in their glen heads and corries more defined climbing-rock is exposed than in any other locale in Scotland outside of Skye, and, notwithstanding the four hundred routes recorded, the area is still far from being exhausted.

Since the war years the corries have been yielding up their secrets and fine routes of major importance have been made. Activity has been such that over two hundred routes recorded in this guide do not appear in the S.M.C. Guide *The Cairngorms*, published in 1950. Many of these are among the finest yet made—reward indeed for the local climber whose faith in the climbing possibilities of the cliffs has been justified despite long-standing accusations against their rock.

All too frequently in the past this has been maligned by climbers with only superficial knowledge of the area. It has been said it is unsound and lacks belays. This may be true of some gully climbs but the buttresses, walls and ridges of honest granite cannot merit this criticism.

Climbers on their first visit to the area will find the climbs typically Scottish in character, completely free from the artificiality which tends to develop in other areas where the cliffs are covered with a network of routes. They will also experience better weather than prevails in other mountain districts. The weather follows an east coast pattern which results in the Cairngorms receiving but half the rainfall allotted to Ben Nevis and Glencoe—a matter of no small importance in an area so ideally suited to the camper-climber. Above all, they will discover that satisfying sense of isolation from the outside world to which climbing in the remote corries gives rise and which in itself is adequate reward.

ROCK FEATURES:
SNOW AND ICE CLIMBING

The rock of the Cairngorms and the Lochnagar–Broad Cairn range is granite, "the best of rocks", basically flesh-pink in colour, but weathering through various shades of greys and browns to a dull black. Weathering also in its more active stages and a heavy glacial action in the past have produced rock structures so diverse in character as to make the climbing in one corrie unlike that in any other. In general however, the rock is rather holdless due to its uniformity of grain and is smooth on north-facing crags but rough when facing south. The climbing is athletic rather than rhythmic—it is never monotonous as the rock demands the use of every technique. Most pitches are more difficult than they appear and the dearth of holds tends to suppress "style" and continuous movement. Friction, pressure and— perhaps most of all—guile are required on the harder routes. Promising lines from below, resolving into unimagined smooth walls and corners above, where a shoulder or a long traverse may be the only ways to success often make route-finding difficult, but this is a recommendation, for in route-finding lies the essence of mountaineering.

Vegetation is present but is usually confined to ledges and grooves on north-facing cliffs; it is avoidable and not troublesome. Lichen on the other hand tends to make the rock greasy in damp and misty conditions, and for this reason it is emphasised that cleated composition soles are often unsuccessful on wet granite.

In the Clova and Glen Isla mountains where the rock

is schist and in Coire Garbhlach in the Cairngorms where gneiss predominates, the climbing is much inferior. These rocks are conducive to a lush vegetable growth, lack definition and in general are too broken to give continuous climbing. Only at Clova, where the rocks are easy of access, do the short climbs become worthwhile.

SNOW AND ICE CLIMBING

Due to their geographical position, the Cairngorms in winter, to misquote one eminent authority, "are the nearest thing we have in Britain to an isolated self-contained range of an almost Arctic type as regards climate". Being influenced more directly by northerly to south-easterly snow-bearing winds than other Scottish mountains their accumulation of snow in any year in comparison is on a vast scale. Because of this build-up, the low mean temperature of the area, height and distance from the sea-boards, their corries retain their snow for an unusually prolonged period, and for this reason magnificent snow and ice work is available during a season which often lasts over seven months of the year. Consequently the development of winter climbing in the area has been great and technique has reached a very high standard.

In view of its comparative ease of access, Lochnagar (not in the Cairngorms massif proper, but strongly allied to it) has been the centre of greatest activity and in its north-east corrie some of Scotland's finest winter routes are found. Here the easier buttresses are transformed into hard problems, the more difficult ridges to climbs of the most exacting nature. The gullies, usually unpleasant summer climbs, come into their own with the development of formidable ice-pitches and giant cornices. Ice however is not confined to the gullies and often forms in quantity over sections of the easier rocks which are grassy in summer and over large areas of the cliff under the plateau rim. It is not easy to compare winter routes on Lochnagar with say, the great Nevis ridges, for although some Nevis climbs are much longer, a major route on Lochnagar may occupy as much time owing to its more sustained difficulty. But comparisons are odious. Both mountains have their own peculiar greatness.

The potential climbs in the Cairngorms proper are legion, but the number of ascents has naturally been limited, due to the remoteness of some of the best corries and the hampering of their approaches by deep snow. The solution appears to lie in a fresh outlook to the use of ski by diehard climbers. These are of inestimable value in cutting out fatiguing snow-wades, even to those whose technique is limited, and also for their speed in communication and adaptability for various purposes in the event of an accident.

Most Scottish mountain accidents in winter are the result of either a blithe indifference shown for objective dangers, an undue faith in axe-belays, inadequate clothing and footgear or complete lack of appreciation of how severe the weather can become. The danger of cornice avalanches in gullies during and after thaw is well known —it is perhaps less well known that they can occur during temperature inversions—but the fact that open-slope avalanches are common in the area, despite the textbooks, and have to be guarded against is not generally appreciated. Pitons for belaying should always be carried; on steep mixed terrain or high-angled gullies axe-belays are virtually useless. Tricounied boots should be worn. Crampons have been used but are not really necessary. It is also to be remembered that in this area with its unusual winter climate, blizzards can last for days and temperatures may sink to levels not normally associated with these Islands. With these facts in mind careful consideration is advisable before climbing from a bivouac in the remote corries in winter. It cannot be stressed too much that the distances to the nearest habitations are great.

A feature of the guide is the introduction of a separate grading system for snow and ice climbs. The editor and his associates have for long believed that the practice of using rock-climbing terms when grading winter climbs was inappropriate and could be misleading—the climber's snow technique often varying greatly from his performance on rock. The system cannot be a hard and fast one—conditions change during a season and from year to year too much for this—but it is felt that it will indicate to the climber more decisively than other methods whether a particular route lies within his power.

NOTES ON THE USE OF THE GUIDE

CLASSIFICATION OF SUMMER ROUTES

The following terms have been used: Easy, Moderate, Difficult, Very Difficult, Mild Severe, Severe, Hard Severe, Very Severe. The letters N.C. indicate that the route, for one reason or another, has not been classified.

An overall grading has been used for the relatively long climbs. They are not graded by their hardest pitches, though in most cases these will correspond. When a pitch exceeds the overall grading it is noted in the text. On some of the sustained severe climbs, insertions have been made in their relative positions in the text to indicate the passages of special difficulty.

The gradings are mostly for nails which are still the best all round wear in the Cairngorms. Vibram soles, which are excellent in dry conditions, are often dangerous in wet weather. A pitch proving too difficult in nails should be climbed in socks. These afford excellent adhesion on granite, especially when damp. An insertion (v.) is made after the grading if the climb is known to have been led in vibrams only.

The classification of the climb is given with each route description and, for easy reference, with the "Index to Climbs" at the end of this volume.

CLASSIFICATION OF WINTER ROUTES

The climbs range from what are easy snow gullies to routes as hard as any in Scotland. Changes in conditions on these climbs do not permit a hard and fast interpretation of the gradings: for instance, gullies whose pitches are uncovered for part of the season may be made easier by subsequent snowfalls, and again, the presence of firm snow on holdless slabs facilitates ascent whereas that of powder increases the difficulty. But the gradings are based on observations of conditions taken over many years and should therefore provide a good indication of what difficulties to expect. Any known variability in the climbs is noted in the text.

GRADE 1. Straightforward, average-angled snow gullies, generally showing no pitches under adequate snow cover. They may, however, present cornice difficulty, or have dangerous outruns in event of a fall. e.g. Central Buttress Gully, Braeriach; South Gully, Beinn a' Bhùird.

GRADE 2. Pitches encountered in gullies, or gullies with high-angle and difficult cornice exits. The easier buttresses which under snow present more continuous difficulty. Reaches a technical standard of Very Difficult. e.g. North-West Gully, Broad Cairn; Central Buttress, Lochnagar.

GRADE 3. Serious climbs which should only be undertaken by parties with good experience. Reaches a technical standard of Severe. e.g. Parallel Gully "A" and Tough–Brown Traverse, Lochnagar.

GRADE 4. Routes which are either of sustained Severe standard or climbs of the highest difficulty which are too short to be classed as Grade 5. e.g. Giant's Head Chimney, Lochnagar; Mitre Ridge, Beinn a' Bhùird; The Stack, Lochnagar (short).

GRADE 5. Routes which give major expeditions and are only to be climbed when conditions are favourable. Technical standard—Very Severe. e.g. Parallel Buttress and Douglas-Gibson Gully, Lochnagar; Sticil Face and Scorpion, Ben Macdhui.

Note: A route climbed between November and May

has not for that reason been admitted to the guide as a winter ascent unless the rocks were snow or ice-bound.

ROPE LENGTHS: One hundred feet between two men is the minimum in the Cairngorms Area.

HEIGHTS: The figures given for climbs are in vertical feet. Several cliffs were measured by aneroid. Elsewhere rope-lengths provided a rough estimate.

LEFT AND RIGHT DIRECTIONS: The terms right and left refer to a climber facing the cliff or upstream.

MAPS: No large-scale map covers the complete area. The ones recommended for use are the One-Inch Ordnance Survey, 7th series, Sheets 37 "Kingussie", and 41 "Braemar".

The term "chokestone" with or without the hyphen is traditional to the area and has been retained.

REFERENCES: The following abbreviations are used:

C.G.	= *Cairngorms Guide* 1950
J.	= *Scottish Mountaineering Club Journal*
C.C.J.	= *Cairngorm Club Journal*
E.C.J.	= *Etchachan Club Journal*
M.M.C.J.	= *Moray Mountaineering Club Journal*
G.C.J.	= *Grampian Club Journal*

Example: J. 4.120 = *Scottish Mountaineering Club Journal* Volume 4, page 120.

THE CAIRNGORMS

ACCESS, ACCOMMODATION AND CAMPING

For the climbs described in Vol. I the best centres are Braemar and Aviemore. Which of the two is selected will depend on the climbs one wishes to perform, and reference should be made to the relevant chapters in this Guide where routes of access to the crags and corries are described. If it is intended to climb both in the Cairngorms and on Lochnagar (see Vol. II) then Braemar should, of course, be chosen. Ballater is a possible alternative centre to Braemar but is rather distant from the Cairngorms being better placed for climbs on Lochnagar.

1. *Braemar.* (Taxi hirers.) Reached from Aberdeen by excellent bus services (Alexander's bus service from Schoolhill and Strachan's Deeside service from Bon-Accord Street each run five buses daily, summer and winter). From Perth a once daily bus service (Alexander's) via the Devil's Elbow operates during the summer months. This service is subject to change but is usually from the beginning of June until the end of September. (N.B. The Perth–Braemar road may remain closed for three months in a winter of heavy snowfall.)

Derry Lodge, the hub of climbing in the Cairngorms, is reached from Braemar by $6\frac{1}{2}$ miles of public and $3\frac{1}{2}$ miles of private road. On this private road there is a locked gate with an opening at the side for motor-cycles. Motorists should apply to Victoria Bridge Cottage $3\frac{3}{4}$ miles from Braemar, for the key, the charge being at the

rate of 2s 6d per day. There may be an increased charge
for taxis and heavier vehicles. Buses are not allowed to
use the road. Keys are withheld during the stalking
season and when the road is soft after thaw.

2. *Aviemore.* (Taxi and bicycle hirers). Reached from
the south by main railway line. Alexander's bus service,
between mid-June and the end of September, operate a
daily long-distance service from Glasgow to Inverness
via Perth and Aviemore. During the winter months this
service runs on Saturdays only. There is also a regular
daily bus service between Newtonmore and Grantown-
on-Spey (Messrs McCormacks, Kingussie).

Loch Morlich Youth Hostel and Glenmore Lodge can
be reached by car through Coylumbridge (6 miles to
Y.H.).

Accommodation

1. *Deeside.* Youth Hostel and hotels at Braemar (and
Ballater). Youth Hostel and boarding houses at Inverey,
5 miles from Braemar. The Cairngorm Club leases Muir
Cottage at Inverey and Derry Lodge for use as Club
Huts. These are open to members of kindred clubs.

The bothies of the Cairngorms are well known and
invaluable. Corrour Bothy, the most famous, lies in
Glen Dee under the Devil's Point. The Hutchison Hut
was constructed in Coire Etchachan in 1954. These are
shelter-huts open to all, built and renovated by the
voluntary labour of climbers, for climbers, and are
excellent bases.

Corrour Bothy has a fireplace and no restrictions; the
Hutchison Hut, by agreement, is locked during the
stalking season. The Etchachan Club (the custodian)
has recently installed a wood- and coal-burning stove.
The other bothies on Deeside are rather far from the
climbing grounds to be of use. For the keen climber

however, there are natural "gîtes" at Loch Avon (Shelter Stone), Coire nan Clach of Beinn a' Bhùird and Garbh Choire Dhàidh of Braeriach. These are described in the appropriate section of the Guide.

2. *Speyside.* Youth Hostel and hotels at Aviemore and Kingussie; Youth Hostel at Loch Morlich. (This Y.H. is the former Glenmore Lodge and is shown as such on the 7th Series O.S. Map. The new Glenmore Lodge belonging to the Scottish Council of Physical Recreation, lies some distance to the east of it.)

Until the erection of the Sinclair Memorial Hut in 1957 at the northern entrance to the Lairig Ghru there were no recognised open shelters for climbers on Speyside, but Ryvoan Bothy and the stable at Petyalach on the Nethy have been used for many years without hindrance. They are private property and climbers who use them have to thank Lady Seafield the owner of the estate and her shooting tenant Mr Naylor for their courtesy in allowing this privilege.

The Sinclair Hut is a two-roomed, solidly built structure situated on a knoll on the right of the Allt Druidh just above a point where the Lairig track, in ascending, crosses from left to right. It has no fireplace or stove. Jean's Hut, in Coire Cas of Cairngorm and the Rothiemurchus Ski Hut below Castle Hill are for the use of Glenmore Lodge S.C.P.R. parties and Services personnel only. Clach Bharraig bothy has been demolished.

CAMPING

The Cairngorms Area is an ideal one for the camper-climber, but on Speyside he is restricted. Camping is not allowed in Glen Einich or in Rothiemurchus or Glenmore Forests. There are public camping grounds near Loch Morlich Y.H. and at Coylumbridge; a charge is made for camping at these sites.

On Deeside a spirit of goodwill has been built up over the years between the estate owners and their stalkers on one hand and the local climbers on the other; camping is permitted within reason almost anywhere. To preserve this friendly relationship, permission to camp should be asked at all times but especially during the stalking season and enquiry should be made as to the likelihood of disturbing a stalk while on the approach to the climb.

Tins, which constitute a grave danger to deer, should be buried.

THE CORRIES OF BEINN A' BHÙIRD
(3924 feet)

BEINN A' BHÙIRD is the highest summit of the Eastern Cairngorms and one of the finest mountains in the country for snow and corrie scenery. It is a remote mountain of vast proportions whose approaches are reckoned to be the most beautiful in the area. Great corries walling an extensive plateau form its eastern front and provide—especially in winter—a scene of great beauty to travellers using the road through the Dee valley.

Only two corries, Coire na Ciche with its characteristic tor, and the expansive Coire nan Clach, are seen from the Braemar approach; the grander Coire an Dubh Lochain, hidden by A' Cioch, and remote Garbh Choire at the head of the Slochd Mòr reserve their charms for the climber and walker.

Apart from minor snow climbs only two routes were recorded previous to the war years; both on the Mitre Ridge in the Garbh Choire. Since then there has been much activity but there is still room for exploration.

APPROACHES

1. *From Braemar* by Aberdeen road (service bus) to gates of Invercauld House. Follow drive and fork right after short distance to upper road by-passing house. Enter Glen an t-Slugain through plantation beyond Alltdourie Cottage. For Coire na Ciche ford the Quoich at the confluence of stream issuing from the corrie. For the Coire an Dubh Lochain and Coire nan Clach keep to the path leading to boulder called Clach à Chléirich, breaking off before final rise to stone. For the Garbh

5

Choire follow stream to the Sneck between Ben Avon and Cnap à Chléirich then contour left avoiding rock-ribs by descending.

2. *From Derry Lodge.* Follow road to Linn of Dee for $1\frac{1}{2}$ miles to watersplash. Go through the pass called Clais Fhearnaig to junction of Quoich and Dubh Ghleann streams. Strike up An Diollaid, a southern spur of Beinn a' Bhùird, to plateau. Easy descents into corries on the north side of each. N.B. This and other direct hill approaches from Derry Lodge must not be used during the stalking season.

3. *From Tomintoul.* Road from Tomintoul to Inchrory for 8 miles (bicycle, no cars without permission), thence follow path on south side of the Avon for $1\frac{1}{2}$ miles. Cross to north side by bridge then $1\frac{3}{4}$ miles to Bruach bothy (ruins). Ford the Avon just beyond the confluence (no bridge as on some maps: spate danger) and for first $1\frac{1}{2}$ miles up the Slochd Mòr hold well to the right to avoid moraines.

CAMPING

The approach by Glen an t-Slugain is the finest and most direct and here there are delectable camping sites in the Fairy Glen below the ruined Slugain Lodge. Permission however must be sought before camping particularly during the stalking season.

COIRE NA CICHE

The symmetrical cup-shaped corrie so well seen from the public road at Invercauld. Several routes have been made on A' Cioch, the great tor rising on the north wall, but though the rock is good the climbing lacks definition. The principal climbs are grouped on the south wall.

On the extreme left is a narrow slabby rib. Trident is on the immediate right of this. Passing rightwards there

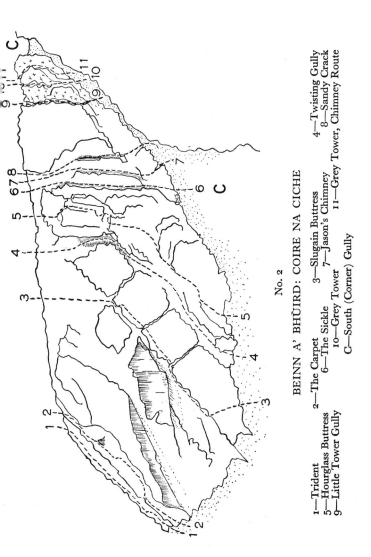

No. 2

BEINN A' BHÙIRD: COIRE NA CICHE

1—Trident   2—The Carpet   3—Slugain Buttress   4—Twisting Gully
5—Hourglass Buttress   6—The Sickle   7—Jason's Chimney   8—Sandy Crack
9—Little Tower Gully   10—Grey Tower   11—Grey Tower, Chimney Route
                       C—South (Corner) Gully

is a great section of slab to the right of a huge alcove in the rock. Up this slab is the Carpet. Further right about the middle of the face and beyond the first break on the cliff (a shallow slanting gully) is Slugain Buttress. Twisting Gully, which has a right-branch ending in a cul-de-sac, separates Slugain Buttress from Hourglass Buttress, the most outstanding feature of the cliff. South Gully, an open shoot terminating the main face, lies at the back of the corrie. Midway up South Gully beyond a steep left branch is the Grey Tower.

The extensive sheet of glaciated slab to the right of South Gully is called Slab Buttress; it is covered with snow in winter to a considerable depth and is liable to avalanche after a heavy build-up.

The rock in the corrie is sound, rough, and very weathered. The climbing tends towards the strenuous and what little vegetation is present must be handled carefully.

The climbs in the corrie are described from left to right:

TRIDENT   330 feet   SEVERE

First ascent: A. Thom and Miss E. Gordon; F. R. Malcolm and Miss S. Anderson   *June 28th 1953*

At the southern end of the face and round a corner to the left of a huge rock alcove and to the right of a slabby rib which appears to be unclimbable.

Start in a groove set in the wall (cairn). Follow groove to a sloping platform tapering sharply to the right. The 12-foot wall ahead is the crux. Climb it by using a shoulder, safeguarded by a piton belay, then follow a slab for 20 feet and traverse left to a flake belay. Take the slab straight ahead using pressure or by layback a few feet to the right. Avoid a vertical wall in front by a traverse right to a belay, thence by a 30-foot moderately inclined slab to piled blocks leading in 75 feet to the plateau.

THE CARPET   300 feet   VERY SEVERE

First ascent: F. R. Malcolm, A. Thom, G. Malcolm,
R. W. P. Barclay and G. Adams   *August 1955*

Starts from the right-hand corner of a grassy recess below and to right of the alcove and goes up a giant slab set in the middle of the upper face. A good route with a fine 100-foot slab pitch.

Climb rightwards up steep slabs and vegetation for 100 feet (care required). From the uppermost grassy ledge the big slab pitch starts with a thin crack. After 50 feet the route trends left to a grass shelf above the slab. The pitch is continuously difficult and quite exposed. (Several pitons used on first ascent—since repeated using two pitons as runners only.) From the grass shelf climb a narrow overhanging cleft by combined effort. A short chimney and a traverse to the right lead to a stance in a crevasse. An easy left traverse gives access to the last pitch—a slab. Either climb in the corner or up a line of dimples on the right edge.

SLUGAIN BUTTRESS   250 feet   DIFFICULT. GRADE 3

First ascent: W. D. Brooker and D. A. Sutherland
                                   August 20th 1949
First winter ascent: G. Adams and D. Macrae
                                   February 10th 1957

The buttress is defined by a slanting groove on the left; halfway up it forms an apex and merges into easy rocks in the upper recess. In winter the route gives a continuous climb of nearly 400 feet. In summer the climb is open to variation and difficulties cease after 250 feet.

Start to the right of the lowest rocks where a rib protrudes between two tiers of a grass ledge (cairn). Climb steep rock to a grooved recess continuing to a grassy shelf. Follow the shelf leftwards and traverse across a flake to the left edge of the buttress. Follow the crest to the apex—a huge, semi-detached block. Go up its right side and then slightly right by the right wall of a diagonal chimney to the easy upper recess.

Winter: On the first ascent normal summer route was followed on hard snow and rocks covered by verglas. The crux was the pitch on the right of the apex-block (pitons). Above this there is a steep snow recess overhung by cornices which gives a good finish to the climb. 350 feet. Time: 4 hours.

TWISTING GULLY   350 feet   MODERATE.   GRADE 2

First winter ascent: K. Milne, J. Davidson and J. Reid
February 28th 1948

The gully twists to the left below a false pinnacle and ends in the easy ground above Slugain Buttress. The right branch is a cul-de-sac. First summer party unknown. There is no special feature in summer but in winter the gully is fairly steep in its lower 200 feet, and the snow recess and cornices above Slugain Buttress give it an excellent finish.

HOURGLASS BUTTRESS   350 feet   VERY SEVERE

First ascent: A. Thom and F. R. Malcolm *May 10th 1953*

The best and hardest route in Coire na Ciche and one of the best in the massif. Above the neck of the Hourglass the climbing is exposed and on perfect rock.

Start at the left corner of the buttress and follow a well-defined groove leading to the neck of the Hourglass. Go up 40 feet of easy rock from the neck to a very steep wall. Climb the wall for 20 feet to a piton belay then traverse right to a crack sloping right. Follow crack to a small rock shelf. The crux follows. This pitch requires a very strenuous pull using a hold high on the left (V.S.), after which easier rock leads to the first substantial platform above the neck. Climb a slightly overhanging crack slanting left (V.S.) and then traverse left to gain a wide crack with an awkward entry finishing the climb.

Variation: A more direct line on the lower part of the Hourglass. Avoid the first tier, then cross on to the buttress from left and climb a steep chimney to a platform in the middle of the face 70 feet below the neck. The next pitch is severe, finishing on the right at the top. (A. O'F. Will and T. W. Patey. April 1955.)

SICKLE   350 feet   VERY DIFFICULT.   GRADE 4

First ascent: W. D. Brooker and D. A. Sutherland
August 21st 1949
First winter ascent: A. Thom and R. Wiseman   *March 1959*

The face between Hourglass Buttress and South Gully is furrowed by three chimneys. Sickle is the leftmost, bounding Hourglass on the right. The central is Jason's Chimney. The rightmost is Sandy Crack.

Enter the chimney by the right wall (cairn) and climb 40 feet to a block belay. Go up a short, steep pitch, then scrambling and a narrow groove to spike belay on wall of Hourglass. The chimney widens to a shallow trough ending in a pair of cracks set in an angle between Hourglass and the wall on the right. Gain a spike belay at the foot of a narrow chimney cleaving this wall by a steep climb of 40 feet, followed by a groove of 20 feet. Climb the chimney for 30 feet to a stance below crux. It is a strenuous pull up on to a flake to the foot of a narrow chimney behind. Continue in the chimney for 12 feet to a chokestone above which the holds improve. From a stance at the top of a flake traverse left to a chimney pitch followed by a further traverse left to a broad shelf on Hourglass. Access to plateau by easy shelf.

Winter: No details available.

JASON'S CHIMNEY   300 feet   SEVERE

First ascent: A. Thom, F. R. Malcolm and A. O'F. Will
October 18th 1953

Start just to the right of Sickle. Follow a shallow groove up easy rock for 120 feet into a deep-cut chimney with a large spike-belay on right wall. Stand on the spike and with the aid of a piton pull up to a rounded ledge and continue up the chimney, or, alternatively, climb close into the back of the chimney by straddling (V.S.). Higher in the chimney turn an overhanging block by a crack on its right which involves an awkward step and pull-up to a grass ledge on right wall. The chimney has now lost its steepness. Climb easy rock for 60 feet and scramble under a large chokestone to the top.

Variation: An earlier attempt on the chimney. The party climbed the rib on the left of the chimney after 30 feet. Defeated at the crux, they entered Sickle on the left and from the stance at the top of the 30-foot chimney on Sickle re-entered Jason's below the overhanging block. (Originally named Rib and Chimney Variation —W. D. Brooker and R. W. McIntyre. August 1949.)

SANDY CRACK   300 feet   VERY DIFFICULT

First ascent: F. R. Malcolm, A. O'F. Will and G. McLeod
August 28th 1955

The rightmost of the long faults. A rather dirty and loose climb. It is best to start a little way up South Gully and traverse back over the Pulpit, a prominent pedestal gained by a steep chimney on the right. An easy descent leads into the fault.

The first big pitch is a very wet chimney with an exit on treacherous sandy ledges (V.D.). The next pitch of 80 feet is of similar standard and gives access to the easy top 60 feet of Jason's Chimney.

SOUTH GULLY   400 feet   GRADE 1

Also named Corner Gully. A scramble in summer. On its steep left wall there are three climbs. In winter it offers an interesting climb often overhung by a large cornice. The sporting exit is up the left hand corner. The first winter party is unknown.

LITTLE TOWER GULLY   200 feet   GRADE 2

First winter ascent: F. R. Malcolm and A. Thom
January 17th 1954

The steep chimney breaking the left wall of South Gully almost forming a branch. It provides a steep climb capped by an awkward cornice. Entry from South Gully can be quite difficult if the build-up of snow is poor. Not a summer climb.

C

GREY TOWER   200 feet   SEVERE

First ascent: A. Thom, F. R. Malcolm and A. O'F. Will
October 18th 1953

This is situated mid-way up South Gully and forms the right wall of Little Tower Gully. The main feature is a large pinnacle well seen when looking up South Gully.

Start to the left of central line (cairn) and climb a few feet of vegetated rock. Continue upwards to a steep 40-foot wall. Take it direct to a belay at top. Easy broken rock to base of the large pinnacle. Approach on its left side and make a strenuous pull-up on small holds to reach a spike belay. Entry to the next pitch is awkward; it is a holdless 20-foot crack topped by a chokestone and is climbed mainly by boot-jamming to the top of the pinnacle. A 10-foot wall finishes the climb.

GREY TOWER, CHIMNEY ROUTE   200 feet
SEVERE

First ascent: F. R. Malcolm, A. O'F. Will and A. Thom
October 18th 1953

Start 50 feet to right of Grey Tower route (cairn). Climb 40 feet of steep rock to belay on left of small cave. Traverse right and move up to a very deep chimney. Climb the chimney until way barred by overhang (stance insecure, piton belay). Take to the right wall and climb on good holds to the top of the chimney and apex of the pinnacle. Finish by last pitch of Grey Tower route.

QUARTZVEIN ROUTE   400 feet   VERY DIFFICULT
GRADE 3

First ascent: Q. T. Crichton and F. L. Swinton
June 30th 1953
First winter ascent: W. A. Christie and J. W. Vigrow
January 1959

This route is on Slab Buttress which presents a concave
face of easy angle in its lower reaches and steepens to an
overhang at the top. The route follows a dyke containing
a vein of quartz. It gives good slab climbing and is
fairly central.

Start at a cairn 25 yards left of lowest rocks. Go up
the vein for 50 feet to a shelf on the right. Continue up
the vein for 70 feet to a small flake belay. Now climb a
10-foot vertical wall to a small recess beneath the overhang. Go up a grass-lined groove on the right and
regain the vein which continues as an exposed, upward
traverse to a fine spike-belay. Continue on the traverse
for 35 feet and finish by slabs.

Winter: On first ascent summer route followed throughout. Ascent of lower snow-covered slabs rapid (crampons). Sustained difficulty for 200 feet on upper rocks
which were iced up.

COIRE AN DUBH LOCHAIN

A noble corrie—in the opinion of many climbers the
most beautiful of the Cairngorm cirques. It is open,
receives much sun, and the view from its floor is wide
and unrestricted. For these reasons it carries a more

cheerful atmosphere than is usual with corries facing
north-east. The Dubh Lochan, from which the corrie
is named, and its satellites lie cupped on its floor
at a height of 3080 feet, backed by cliffs 600 feet in
height.

There is less climbing than the area of crag suggests.
Broken rock is the feature of the slope leading to A' Cioch
on the left skyline. In the centre above the main lochan
the rocks at the base are indefinite, but small buttresses
appear high up with defined gullies between, giving
good winter climbing. The main climbs are on two
imposing buttresses which lie above the smaller lochans
in the S.W. corner. These buttresses are separated by a
long scree-shoot—the Main Rake. Bloodhound Buttress
on the left has a very steep wall dropping into the Rake.
At half-height in the Rake, this wall is cut by Tantalus
Gully. Glaucous Buttress is the broad-based crag to the
right of the Rake, composed of curious pillars and
grooves and a large area of slab, topped by steep ram-
parts. Most routes are on this buttress. To the west of
this in winter is a huge field of snow, named the Avalanche Slope.

The face between the depression in the plateau west
of A' Cioch and Bloodhound Buttress is divided vertically by A and B gullies, open-walled depressions 500
feet in height. Both give straightforward winter climbs.
It is not possible to determine which was followed by
Garden, Goodeve, Ling, Raeburn and Watson, in April
1908 (J. 10.148). They are not summer routes. The rib
dividing the gullies affords better winter climbing. The
central of three small buttresses under the plateau left
of A gully has been climbed (150 feet. Moderate. K.
Winram and C. Petrie, July 1950)—the rightmost forming the upper left wall of A gully is Smooth Buttress.
Though short, this should give a good climb.

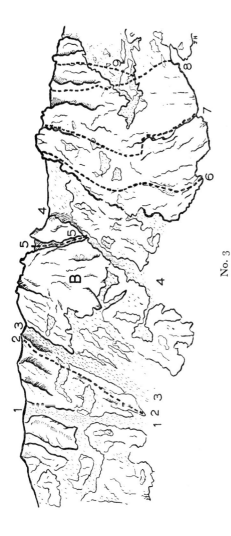

No. 3

COIRE AN DUBH LOCHAIN, BEINN A' BHÙIRD

1—A Gully
2—Winter Rib
3—B Gully
4—The Main Rake
5—Tantalus Gully

6—May Day Route
7—Polypody Groove
8—Crow-Step Route
9—Birthday Route
B—Bloodhound Buttress

A AND B GULLIES   500 feet   GRADE 1

No pitches. Steep exits with heavy cornices usually entire.

WINTER RIB   500 feet   GRADE 2

First Ascent: J. Tewnion, G. Dey and M. Smith
November 26th 1950

Rib is composed of easy-angled broken rock ending in three small upper buttresses. The rightmost continuing the original line was followed. Steep rock. A graduating climb.

Bloodhound Buttress. This imposing buttress throws down a short inclined wall of slab into the upper reaches of B gully, but its finest feature is the 300-foot wall dropping into the Main Rake. The bolsters and slabs of ash-grey granite making up this face are uncompromising —there are few horizontal joints. The only climb made so far was completed with the aid of a top rope for one pitch. Although it is uncertain whether a genuine ascent could be made, the following account is worth recording. "The start was 80 feet below Tantalus Gully and worked up and leftwards to a curious arch of jammed blocks. Then 40 feet of rock led to a steep crack harbouring some grass tufts. The crack gave 20 feet of V.S. climbing to a small stance. Another V.S. move was made out and over a holdless slab on the right to a comfortable platform. Two cracks were then attempted, one straight ahead, the other round a corner to the right. Both were initially V.S. and required a top rope to complete them. Easier ground led to the top up a prominent depression. Holds on the climb were often obscured by tufts of vegetation. This added to the difficulty." (T. W. Patey and W. W. Hutchison, September 1953.)

TANTALUS GULLY   250 feet   SEVERE.   GRADE 3

First ascent: G. C. Greig, M. Smith and K. Winram
March 15th 1953

First winter ascent: R. Ellis and M. Scott *February 10th 1957*

This is the first break in the wall of Bloodhound Buttress, about midway up the Main Rake. There is little evidence of gully form in the first two pitches, but higher up it cuts deep into the mountain and is contained by high walls.

Go up broken rock for 30 feet to a stance below the first pitch—a 15-foot overhang with a smooth slab on the right. The key handhold to this strenuous pitch is tucked in a slot behind the overhang (S.) A waterworn groove follows to the second pitch; steep rounded slabs best climbed in the right corner (M.S.). The angle then eases to a third pitch again on waterworn slabs (20 feet). The fourth pitch culminating in a huge scree funnel is started on the left and finished on the right under piled blocks (25 feet).

Winter: The gully varies in difficulty, but will always be fairly hard under genuine conditions. The initial pitch may be banked for some of its height, but usually combines with its continuation to form one long pitch which will provide a long bout of one-handed cutting on high-angled ice (45 feet on first ascent). The upper gully is straightforward though often well corniced. Time on first ascent: 3½ hours.

MAIN RAKE   500 feet   GRADE 1

First winter ascent: H. Alexander, A. A. Longden and
A. M. Watt   *April 1911*

No pitches in summer. Under snow the angle is not excessive. Cornice generally easy. Do not glissade without knowing the conditions lower down; the rake slants and there is a tendency to be pushed in a straight line on to slabs running parallel with the rake, and rising imperceptibly from it.

Glaucous Buttress

The green lower slabs of this important buttress have different aspects on each side of a long central break. On the left side there is a series of smooth granite pillars with their attendant grooves each the counterpart of the other. The right side is a 250-foot sweep of holdless slab. The line of demarcation is Polypody Groove. Above the lower slabs a series of small upper ribs is divided vertically by thin, converging chimneys. May Day Route is on the ridge of rock bounding the Main Rake. Crow-Step and Birthday Routes are on subsidiary buttresses to the right of the main mass.

MAY DAY ROUTE   600 feet   DIFFICULT

First ascent: J. Tewnion, E. L. Smith, W. A. Russell and
M. Smith   *May 1st 1949*

Start in a groove to left of lowest rib (cairn). The groove continues as a shelf inclining right. 120 feet up move to the left and go up an awkward groove. Above, it is a scramble up an ill-defined ridge to more interesting rocks at the top.

POLYPODY GROOVE   600 feet   MILD SEVERE

First ascent: J. Tewnion and E. L. Smith *August 21st 1949*

This popular route lies up the break separating the pillared section from the slab section of the lower buttress. From the corrie floor it appears as a dark slanting shadow with two zig-zag overhangs high up. The climbing is on clean rock. Due to lack of time on the first ascent, the upper continuation chimney was not followed and previous diagrams show the route diverging to upper May Day Route. The continuation was climbed by F. R. Malcolm and A. Thom in 1952 (V.D.). This is the route now followed.

The lower section of the groove may be resolved into pitches: 50 feet easy going to a block belay, 50 feet up smooth rock on the right to a belay stance and 80 feet of delicate friction climbing (V.D.) to an overhang (runner). Above the overhang follow the groove for 100 feet to a belay. The groove now steepens and becomes holdless. Traverse out of it to the left and climb a small pitch to a ledge. The next problem is to reach and stand on a rounded hold 8 feet up a rib on the left (M.S.) to avoid the next overhang. 20 feet of hard climbing leads to an upper terrace. Follow a line slightly rightward towards the deepest and most obvious of the chimneys in the upper rampart. Scrambling for most of the way, but two steep pitches must be climbed before traversing across a slab above the chokestone. Easy above to plateau.

Winter: The 300-foot lower section is completely masked by a snowfield; Polypody Groove as such does not exist. Even the pillars fail to show. A true bergschrund forms at the head of the slabs. Ascents have been made in these conditions finished by traversing to upper May Day Route. The obvious winter climb is the combination of lower May Day Route and upper continuation of Polypody Groove.

CROW-STEP ROUTE   550 feet   VERY DIFFICULT

First ascent: C. Petrie and M. Smith   *August 21st 1949*

Start some yards to the right of Polypody Groove past

the waterslide coming over the great slab (cairn). 300 feet of easy to moderate climbing on stepped slabs leads to the 250-foot upper buttress. Start on this near the centre by a strenuous 15-foot pitch formed by a flake set into a shallow chimney topped by an overhanging block. From a stance make an upward movement to the left then pull up over the crest to slabs with rounded holds leading to a mossy platform. Step up to a ledge and belay. Go round a corner on the left and climb a series of ribs against the left wall of the buttress and regain the crest by a 15-foot pitch. Scramble up an arête to the plateau.

BIRTHDAY ROUTE   200 feet   MILD SEVERE

First ascent: K. A. Grassick, J. G. Lillie and R. Preshaw
June 7th 1952

A number of parallel chimneys cut the depression between Crow-Step and a small pointed buttress breaking the skyline on the extreme right of Glaucous Buttress. Counting from Crow-Step, Birthday Route is the third of these chimneys. Reach it by climbing the first section of Crow-Step.

Climb the first pitch on the right wall to avoid an overhang and regain the chimney by an awkward move left. Ledges lead to a stance and belay. Avoid an overhang on the second pitch by working up on the left and by an easy right traverse gain a rock mass. The chimney narrows. A straddle stance is reached with difficulty in 60 feet. The chimney now merges into the face. The last 60-foot pitch is climbed on the left by a narrow crack between two walls. Gain the culminating wall of 10 feet below the plateau by an awkward move round a chokestone and climb the wall itself by an out-of-balance move on the left and a strenuous pull-up.

COIRE NAN CLACH

Though containing less rock than the other corries, Coire nan Clach with its extensive floor and chaos of boulders should attract the climber with its beauty and air of seclusion. The summit of Beinn a' Bhùird lies a short distance from the edge of the corrie. The best climbs are on the Dividing Buttress, the impressive bastion which separates the Dubh Lochain corrie from Coire nan Clach. As seen from the Quoich approach the ridge falling to the rim of Coire an Dubh Lochain is Slab and Arête. The right skyline is Sentinel Route. Between these routes are glaciated slabs, low-angled at the base but steep and holdless higher up. At the back of the corrie a rock promontory contains two short climbs.

In winter the corrie is ringed by a continuous cornice and gives good straightforward climbing especially on the wall running west from the Dividing Buttress. Four good gullies of 500–600 feet are found here running up through the small upper buttresses. Of these the right-most, which is called Crocus Gully, is the better and more defined. All are Grade 1 climbs.

Bivouac Smith-Winram is a built-up recess under the second largest boulder immediately below the glabrous slabs on Dividing Buttress. The accommodation is rough (capacity 3) but it is ideal for a long visit. The surroundings are magnificent. Sentinel Route is only 10 minutes away—Glaucous Buttress in Coire an Dubh Lochain 30 minutes. The time to the Garbh Choire approached by the stream issuing from Cnap a' Chléirich is 45 minutes.

Dividing Buttress

The climbing here is less good than would appear likely on viewing the crag from a distance. The rock on the left bordering a large scree shoot is very broken. The only climb here is Slab and Arête which lies to the left of this shoot, forming a flying ridge to the buttress—the true dividing line between the corries. On the right the smooth slabs flanking Sentinel Route at mid-height have given very difficult indefinite routes of 100–120 feet and could give more, but those are ultra-short. Sentinel Route is a long rib bounded on the right by Sentinel Gully. Across this gully and forming a gable to the buttress is another rib, thin in its lower part and widening above a glacis into a fine, upper, unclimbed bulge.

SLAB AND ARÊTE   450 feet   MODERATE

First ascent: J. Tewnion and M. Smith   *April 4th 1948*

The dividing line between the corries. A pleasant romp amid grand scenery for a short day or in poor weather. Popular.

To get the best out of the climb start at the bottom right-hand corner. Here are some interesting cracked slabs. About mid-way the ridge rises to a false tower above a scooped slab. Go up a central chimney or by a split bulge on the extreme left to a short arête.

SENTINEL ROUTE   500 feet   DIFFICULT

First ascent: K. Winram and M. Smith   *May 28th 1949*

On a rib forming the right skyline. A steep, defined route between smooth slabs on the left and Sentinel Gully on the right.

Start by scrambling for 100 feet over low-angled slabs to the first pitch (cairn). A steep 80-foot groove ends in a corner overlooking the gully. Make an exposed traverse to the right to a belay. Continue up a short wall to a low-angled groove and a stretch of slabs. Thence follow a rib straight ahead to a huge boss of rock on the plateau.

Sentinel Gully is uninteresting in summer. It has two pitches. In winter it should give fair sport. 250 feet unclimbed.

The Promontory

Coire nan Clach is itself divided into two lobes by a promontory. The lobes become huge snowfields rimmed by great cornices in winter and the promontory gives two short climbs in summer:

PROMONTORY GULLY   200 feet   MODERATE

First ascent: K. Winram and M. Smith   *May 28th 1949*

Starting about 20 feet above the screes the gully comprises the following features: 15-foot moderate pitch, a long V groove topped by an overhang, a large chokestone and finally a 30-foot optional pitch in the left branch.

WALL AND SLAB   200 feet   DIFFICULT

First ascent: K. Winram, J. Tewnion and E. L. Smith
May 29th 1949

This climb lies up the left side of Promontory Gully. Start from a grass platform at the foot of the gully and climb a hanging scoop to a grass ledge. Climb a crack in a slab slanting left and then right to another platform. Thence climb the corner overlooking the gully. Heathery slabs follow.

GARBH CHOIRE

Lying north of the watershed the enchanting Garbh Choire forms the headwall of the Slochd Mòr (Muckle Slock) a fine valley deep-set between Ben Avon and Stob an t-Sluichd and sending a feeder stream to the Avon. An air of secrecy must be added to its remote atmosphere; for on all approaches the cliffs remain hidden until the actual corrie is entered.

The cliffs have a maximum height of 650 feet. The rock is rough and generally sound but the more enticing jughandles should be used judiciously.

The features of the corrie are two superb buttresses at each end of the main face. These are Squareface and the Mitre Ridge. Between them a stretch of cliff of lesser character contains many gullies. One of these, the Flume, encloses a large stream—a good pointer in thick weather. To the right of the main face the continuity of the cliff is interrupted by a wide, gravelly depression beyond which a series of miniature arêtes run up to the backbone of Stob an t-Sluichd.

The Mitre Ridge, named from its resemblance to a bishop's mitre, aroused great interest before its ascent by two parties in 1933. This splendid crag with its plinth of furrowed slabs supporting three jagged upper towers is rock architecture at its best. It is now a classic climb by either of its original routes.

Squareface gives one of the best routes in the area. The climb wends its way up an apparently holdless wall of 330 feet set at high angle, by a series of delightfully exposed traverses on impeccable granite.

From the Sneck on the left to Squareface the rocks are fairly continuous and form a scarp of ribs which descend low into the corrie as they approach its centre. The ribs

No. 4

GARBH CHOIRE, BEINN A' BHÙIRD

1—Squareface
2—Back Bay Gully
3—Laminated Crag
4—Approach Gully
5—Consolation Gully
6—The Flume
7—Mandarin Buttress
S—The Sneck

8—South-East Gully
9—East Wall Direct, Mitre Ridge
10—Direct Route, Mitre Ridge
11—Alternative Start, Direct Route, Mitre Ridge
12—Cumming-Crofton Route, Mitre Ridge
13—Commando Route, Mitre Ridge
14—North-West Gully
C—Summit of Cnap a' Chléirich

are somewhat ill-defined and without recorded routes. At their lowest point, to the left of a wide scree-shoot, they run up to the blank, vertical north wall of Square-face (the west wall on which the climb is situated is hidden from below). At its head the shoot opens out into an amphitheatre hemmed in on the left by the west wall of Squareface—the High Bay. From the Bay easy ground goes up rightwards to the plateau. For the routes in the Bay and approaching from the plateau this is handier for a descent than the gravel slopes west of Mitre Ridge which would entail a subsequent tiring ascent.

The routes from the High Bay

SQUAREFACE   330 feet   VERY DIFFICULT

First ascent: T. W. Patey and J. M. Taylor   *July 1953*

A narrow gully with one prominent chokestone runs up along the rectangular west wall between it and a crag at the head of the Bay. The route starts from the foot of the gully on the right side of an arête which drops from the apex of the north and west walls, climbs to the arête, then continues up the apparently holdless slab. One of the best climbs in the massif. The rock is superb and the climbing absolutely continuous. Two lengthy exposed leads are required.

Start just round the corner of the arête and climb 100 feet to a large platform on the edge. Go 30 feet up the arête to a stance (piton belay) below an overhang. Launch out onto the wall by a 30-foot slab traverse, past the first obvious vertical crack until it is possible to climb straight up and return left to a platform on the edge at 90 feet. Go on to the face once more and follow cracks up to the right for 30 feet to a short horizontal crack.

Six feet on the right a deep fissure cleaves the final section. Jam up this for 12 feet then leave it for a shelf on the right, thence gain the top by a delicate upward traverse.

BACK BAY GULLY   350 feet   DIFFICULT. GRADE 2

First ascent: G. C. Greig, M. Smith and K. Winram
August 24th 1952
First winter ascent: T. W. Patey, G. B. Leslie, A. G. Nicol and J. M. Taylor   *March 31st 1954*

The narrow gully ascending to the plateau close under the wall of Squareface.

Moderate climbing on waterworn rock for 100 feet leads to a cave below a chokestone. Turn the boulder on the left wall by an awkward slab with small holds and continue up the gully narrowing with height and again on waterworn rock to a fork. Ascend the left hand groove.

Winter: Late in the season it is a uniform snow slope, but heavily corniced and high-angled. The first party found 70° snow for some distance below the cornice which was turned on the left.

LAMINATED CRAG   250 feet   VERY DIFFICULT

First ascent: K. Winram and M. Smith   *March 8th 1953*

The squat crag at the head of the Bay forming the right wall of Back Bay Gully.

The crag presents a broad front. Near the centre of the wall climb a short pitch to a transverse level shelf extending the whole width of the crag. At the left end a huge flake slants up to the right. Climb this "à cheval" for 30 feet and enter a level-floored crevasse. Surmount a short vertical step with few handholds to a niche (V.D.) then traverse back and upwards to the left by a series of

D

mantelshelves to a belay. The next pitch goes rightwards up to a pointed flake in two steps. Easy ground
follows.

————————

BETWEEN the shoot leading to High Bay and the Flume is
a big area of crag, steep in its lower half and highest at
its centre. It is crowned by a belt of vegetation. Above
this again a margin of rock forms a frieze under the
plateau.

The steep lower half has a small 200-foot buttress
bordering the right side of the shoot. Although artificial,
this gives the best route to the Bay from the corrie floor.
Started at the centre, the initial pitches give good and
hard climbing (G. Malcolm and R. W. P. Barclay, 1954).
Approach Gully, a slanting gully, goes up the right side
of this buttress and exits level with the foot of Back Bay
Gully. A wet scramble in summer—in winter it is often
straightforward but as often contains ice in quantity.
Combined with Back Bay Gully (as by the first party)
this gives a long continuous climb to the plateau.

The next definite feature is Consolation Gully lying
centrally.

CONSOLATION GULLY 400 feet VERY DIFFICULT
GRADE 2

First ascent: J. Tewnion and K. Winram *July 30th 1950*
First winter ascent: T. W. Patey, R. H. Sellers and R.
    Harper   *April 15th 1956*

Climb a moderate pitch over slabs and piled blocks
and enter the gully. The first pitch is smooth, wet and
mossy; the second starts with a 20-foot chimney with a
good stance on top. Climb the chokestone above on the

left. The third pitch is 100 feet long, but is easier. No great difficulty to the top.

Winter: Often straightforward though steep, easing to plateau, but more often presenting an ice-pitch in the long chimney. (40 feet on first ascent.)

THE FLUME 600 feet GRADE 2

First ascent (winter): J. M. Taylor and G. B. Leslie
March 31st 1954

The channel gouged in the cliff by the Allt an t-Sluichd already a lusty stream on the plateau before it drops over the edge. The gully is open-walled and ends in a high waterfall pitch under the plateau. It is not a summer climb. At the start of the gully a dirty, right fork opens on to slabs on Mandarin Buttress, the next climb to the right.

In winter the main gully is straightforward up to a huge ice-pitch (the summer waterfall). The difficulty lies in threading a way between this and a big ice-pitch which forms in the left-hand exit. The long upward traverse between the pitches is quite difficult if the build-up of snow is poor.

MANDARIN BUTTRESS 600 feet DIFFICULT

First ascent: T. W. Patey and A. Watson; K. Winram and
M. Smith *August 29th 1954*

The buttress between the Flume and South-East Gully of Mitre Ridge. Above a steep lower section there is a broad terrace from which a defined arête continues to the plateau.

Follow a fault on the right side of the buttress gained by a steep pitch alongside South-East Gully or by easy ledges from the left. At the top of the fault cut back left

by short walls to the terrace (300 feet). The upper
arête affords good climbing on clean rock to a great,
square block perched athwart the ridge.

The Mitre Ridge

One of the finest pieces of rock architecture in the
massif. It thrusts up boldly between its gullies, 650 feet
from scree to plateau in two walls meeting at an acute
angle and topped by three massive towers. The West
Wall is vertical, the East less steep but slabby and
smooth, scored by grooves and cracks.

The Ridge was named by J. A. Parker and prospected
by him and Drummond in 1921. Parker's enthusiasm
for the Ridge led to his encouraging parties to try its
ascent and it had aroused considerable interest before
falling to two parties on the same day by different routes
in the remarkable summer of 1933.

There are now seven routes including its gullies.

From left to right these are:

SOUTH-EAST GULLY   500 feet   VERY DIFFICULT
GRADE 5

First ascent: J. Hunt and A. Y. Greenhalgh   *June 1943*
First winter ascent: R. H. Sellers and G. Annand
February 1959

The gully bounding the Ridge on its left. One of the
better Cairngorm gullies; it is shallow and slabby and
pitons should be carried for belaying.

Start from the highest ground at its foot.

After 40 feet of awkward holdless slabs (V.D.) continue by steep climbing on good holds on the left of the
main watercourse to a comfortable platform 100 feet
from the start. Scramble right to the next major obstacle
—a very long V-groove. The first 60 feet in the groove

is steep (V.D.) then it eases off and is grass-filled. From top of groove more steep climbing leads to a point where it is advisable to traverse left and reach easy ground in the gully above. Easy slopes now to the last great pitch. This is 180 feet high, climbed in three pitches each increasing in difficulty as one proceeds. The last 80 feet (S.) on disintegrating rock is somewhat dangerous and best skirted by a detour on the right wall (D.). Easy scrambling to the top.

Winter: Forms a most beautiful couloir of singularly alpine appearance—wide, shallow and very steep. Conditions vary but it will always be very hard. First party found a 40-foot ice-groove in lower gully, then 120 feet of snow to the point where East Wall Route leaves the gully. From here to the summit there was a succession of fine ice-pitches providing magnificent climbing. Time: 4 hours.

EAST WALL ROUTE   600 feet   GRADE 4

First ascent: T. W. Patey and A. G. Nicol *March 31st 1954*

A fine winter route; the outcome of an attempt on South-East Gully abandoned through the onset of a sudden thaw. From the point of abandonment in the gully the route deviated rightwards up the East Wall of the Ridge to join the Direct Route at the top of the second Tower (start of level section of final arête).

The initial 140 feet of the gully was obliterated. An 80-foot pitch on snow-ice led to an easier slope. At the point where the left traverse is made in summer the gully was left by a direct ascent of the right wall and steep snow (vegetated rock in summer) traversed upwards to the right to the foot of an ice-couloir. On the right a holdless chimney ascended to the col between the first and second Towers. This appeared to be too hard

No. 5

MITRE RIDGE—EAST FACE

1—Mandarin Buttress   3a—Easy Traverse to Direct Route
2—South-East Gully   4 —East Wall Route
3—East Wall Direct   5 —Direct Route

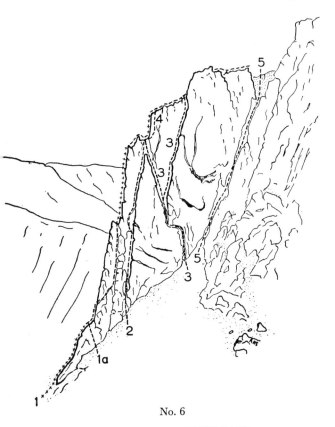

No. 6

MITRE RIDGE—WEST FACE

1 —Direct Route	3—Commando Route
1a—Alternative Start	4—Bell's Variation
2 —Cumming-Crofton Route	5—North-West Gully

so the couloir was entered. Continuously severe ice-work for 60 feet required two pitons for security and ended at a belay just beyond an awkward tilt. A break in the right wall 20 feet higher provided a difficult exit and led to an exposed nose. On the far side a descent of 12 feet revealed a wide 20-foot chimney. Although not iced this was severe. Mixed rock and snow led to the top of the second Tower. Time: 3 hours.

EAST WALL DIRECT   650 feet   MILD SEVERE

First ascent: T. W. Patey   *August 29th 1954*

Combines the ascent of the lower slabs with that of the upper couloir used in winter on the East Wall Route. The route follows an almost direct line from its start to the final, third, Tower of the Ridge.

Start up the widest of the cracks which cleave the slabs midway between South-East Gully and the lowest point of the Ridge. The crack is steep for 50 feet but the holds are good. The angle lessens and there is no difficulty in the crack as it cuts through the sweep of slabs. The way is barred at the top by a line of overhangs. A deep crack splits them directly above, but a smooth slab acts as an effective moat. Lodgement in the crack is gained by an awkward straddle from a minor crack on the right (M.S.). The deep crack itself goes more easily and the continuation follows a line of grassy chimneys with good holds on the side walls, but the uppermost is too wide and has to be straddled. (Here one can pass right behind a detached block and by easy terraces gain the shoulder of the Ridge.)

Continuing directly upwards 200 feet of mixed climbing with some awkward moves leads to the "winter couloir". Ascend the couloir (D. in summer) for 60 feet to block belay. The winter exit 20 feet above looks too

hard without a snow take-off. Instead climb the rib on
the left, passing just left of the overhangs ringing the top
of the couloir (V.D.). Easy gully on right to final col,
but the best finish is straight ahead up the continuation
of the rib to the top of the final Tower.

DIRECT ROUTE   650 feet   GRADE 4
    VERY DIFFICULT (avoiding the initial groove)
    HARD SEVERE (inclusive, in nails)

First ascent: E. A. M. Wedderburn, P. D. Baird and
    E. J. A. Leslie   *July 4th 1933*
First winter ascent: W. D. Brooker and T. W. Patey
    April 2nd 1953

The first pitch (110 feet) is divorced from the rest of
the climb in the grading to encourage more parties to
make the ascent of an excellent route. The initial groove,
however, is one of the classic Cairngorms pitches and
should not be missed by a competent party.

The groove is obvious, midway between the lowest
rocks and the corner of the buttress (cairn). Holdless
slabs at 55° with an overhanging wall on the left require
a run-out of 110 feet. The slabs are topped by a 7-foot
wall, overhanging slightly but with adequate holds
allowing a pull-up to a small stance (strenuous). In 50
feet a better stance is reached where the easy route joins
from the right (this, which provides quite a logical start,
goes up a line of weakness at the corner of the Ridge.
C. Ludwig and D. J. Dawson, September 1933. Moderate). Continue to follow the rising shelf slanting round
the Ridge, first by a short, easy chimney and ending
below a deep-cut chimney of 40 feet blocked by an overhang. Climb the chimney, which belies its forbidding
appearance, well out (D.). A shallow 40-foot gully now
leads to a shoulder on the Ridge (cairn).

A delicate balance traverse to the right, then steep rock for 90 feet brings one to the foot of the steep wall below the first Tower. To gain a broad, grassy ledge there are two alternatives:

(*a*) The most direct way—a 15-foot inset, right-angled corner (V.D.).

(*b*) Move left across a grassy slab (piton safeguard in the corner) and ascend a splintered chimney (D.–V.D.).

From the ledge the pioneers ascended the Tower directly, but most parties now appear to climb the wall above the ledge and ascend to the narrow col between the first and second Towers.

The second Tower can be turned on the left (D.) or ascended by a steep crack on the face but the finest route is by—

Bell's Variation: Follow a shelf to the right corner and climb a steep crack on the west face. When this peters out, step left and finish straight up (V.D. exposed).

The finish to the climb lies along a narrow, sensational arête for 70 feet over the final tower. (J. 20.184, 458.)

Winter: On the first ascent the Ridge was plastered with snow after a heavy fall. Extensive clearing of holds was necessary, even on the steeper pitches. The initial groove was by-passed (it should give little trouble under hard snow). The 40-foot chimney was heavily iced and was turned on the right. Defeated at the delicate traverse the party overcame the wall directly by combined tactics. At the base of the first Tower, variant (*b*) was used (crux). The next pitch to the col was also very hard, and the second Tower turned on the left. The final arête was a most impressive finish. Time: 4½ hours.

THE WEST WALL

Vertical, indeed overhanging in places. The only lines of weakness are two corners or gullies which run up on either side of a curious 350-foot subsidiary triangular buttress which stands out from the wall of the Ridge. The corners meet behind the top of the subsidiary which rests against the Ridge above the first Tower. Cumming-Crofton Route follows the left-hand corner on the arête between the first and second Towers; Commando Route the right-hand corner to a point where it forks—the left fork joining the top of Cumming-Crofton, the right fork, which is longer, running up to the final col on the Ridge.

Close into the corner of West Wall is North-West Gully, which is bounded on the right by a broken buttress.

CUMMING-CROFTON ROUTE 350 feet to the arête
SEVERE

First ascent: M. S. Cumming and J. W. Crofton
July 4th 1933

The finest route on the Ridge and one of the best in the Cairngorms. The climbing is continuously difficult and exposed, seldom less than Very Difficult in standard. Dry conditions recommended.

Start directly below the corner and go straight up 25 feet to a small shelf. Above is a prominent, dark chimney. Climb the chimney which has a hanging flake forming a constriction at mid-height (M.S.). A fine stance in a cleft at the top. (The route here is only 20 feet from the Direct Route at a point above the chimney on the latter; it is easy to cross from one to the other). Traverse rightwards for 30 feet by the way of a short, holdless groove. When stopped by a vertical wall return left by an airy traverse across a wall and round a holdless corner (S. exposed). Small spike belay.

The general line is now up the corner between the

Ridge and the subsidiary. For the first 15 feet climb just to the right of the crack beneath the wall of the main ridge to an excellent running belay (S. crux). Step left into crack and climb to a broad platform at 80 feet (piton belay). Climb a crack in the left wall then traverse right and follow a sloping ledge to a belay projecting from the wall.

Pursuing the same line follow a loose gully for 80 feet to reach the arête between the first and second Towers. Bell's Variation is the logical continuation.

COMMANDO ROUTE   450 feet by the Right Fork
VERY DIFFICULT

First ascent: Sgt.-Major Langlands and A. D. M. Cox
June 1943
(This is Route II of Cairngorms Guide 1950)

Start just below the foot of North-West Gully. The difficulty is to get started on the corner which does not begin until 70 feet up. It is reached by an exposed traverse from a minor gully on the right. The traverse involves the use of a trick move, utilising an undercut hold, but it can be protected safely from above. Round the corner the next few feet upwards are fairly hard, but after this there is little difficulty up to the fork. The left fork to the top of the subsidiary buttress is an easy scramble; the longer right fork is more interesting and has three long indefinite pitches (D.) leading to the final col on the Ridge.

Winter: No ascent recorded. It should provide an excellent climb but would require a heavy bank-up on the first pitch to facilitate entry to the corner. Thereafter the long right fork would give first-class climbing.

NORTH-WEST GULLY 350 feet DIFFICULT. GRADE 3

First visited on descent: Sgt.-Major Langlands and A. D. M.
    Cox   *June 1943*
First ascent: M. Smith and J. Tewnion *September 19th 1948*
First winter ascent: R. H. Sellers and G. Adams
                                              December 16th 1956

Quite a pleasant gully climb—good, clean rock and
no watercourse.

The start is up a steep 15-foot wall followed by large
boulders. Waterworn slabs lead to a chimney in the
Ridge wall. Go up a crack in the slab on the right and
follow a continuation groove past a small chokestone
to a belay stance. Another chimney cuts deep into the
Ridge wall. Climb the rib forming the right wall of the
chimney and cross into a depression in the slabs to the
right and up to a small belay. The final pitch is short
and is again a crack in the slabs leading to a scree funnel.

Winter: The approach from the corrie floor is by a
graceful arête of snow which swings up steeply round the
base of the Ridge. The gully itself varies greatly in difficulty. All will depend on the time of visit and the
accumulation of snow in the right-angled funnel at its
head. This acts as a reservoir so that with alternate
thawing and freezing after a good build-up, a cascade of
clear ice 100 feet in height may form feet thick on the
slabs (April 1954). The first party found easy conditions
immediately after blizzard—2 hours of high-angled step-
cutting on hard-packed snow.

The small buttress bounding North-West Gully on the
right has been climbed by various parties. Ascent is
possible at various points.

STOB AN T-SLUICHD

This top of Beinn à Bhùird sports a fine array of miniature arêtes and buttresses which face across to the Mitre Ridge and get the sun most of the day. At their maximum they are 250 feet in height. The climbing is of a carefree, sporting nature on rough rock. All that is worthwhile has been climbed, and although each gives good pitches detailed description is not called for.

Only the most defined one and the largest have been named.

PINNACLE RIDGE   250 feet   DIFFICULT

First ascent: G. W. Ross and A. E. Anton   *July 4th 1948*

The best defined and at the left-hand end of the group. It slopes slightly left and ends in a pinnacle seen against the sky. Developing quickly into a narrow, defined arête and steep on its western side it maintains its interest right to the top.

BETWEEN Pinnacle Ridge and the buttress on the extreme right there are four more or less defined arêtes. All were climbed by ascent or descent in July 1950 (C. Petrie and K. Winram). Interesting but much artificiality.

M AND B BUTTRESS   250 feet   MODERATE

First ascent: G. Mathieson and I. M. Brooker
May 28th 1949

The broader buttress on the extreme right beyond a wide shoot. Easy on its right edge. Better climbing, starting up the centre by rough slabs, then scrambling only.

COIRE SPUTAN DEARG OF
BEN MACDHUI

ONE of the finest moments afforded when traversing the
Lairig Ghru—especially in winter and spring—occurs
when Glen Luibeg is first seen stretching north through
all its length to the eastern top of Ben Macdhui called
Stob Coire Sputan Dearg. A ridge falling from this bold
peaked summit is then seen as the dividing line between
two corries; the snow-walled Coire Lochan Uaine to the
south and the grander Coire Sputan Dearg with its file
of black buttresses and snow-filled gullies on the north.

Coire Sputan Dearg is perhaps the most popular corrie
in the Cairngorms outside of Lochnagar and might well
be termed a "playground". The reason for this attraction lies mainly in its comparative accessibility, but the
corrie also faces south-east, gets much sun, and the
climbs, though not exceeding 450 feet, are on rock that
is everywhere excellent—rough, clean and sound.

Unaccountably, the rocks of the corrie aroused no
interest until 1948. The deterrent may well have been
the statement made in a previous guide that "the rock is
unsuited for climbing". Changes are wrought by the
years!—for the novice on granite there is no better
training ground than Coire Sputan Dearg.

APPROACHES

1. *From Derry Lodge.* Follow the Lairig Ghru track for
2 miles and fork right up a steep rising path some 150
yards short of the Luibeg burn. Higher up near the
Sron Riach, the path becomes indistinct. Follow either
bank; one has no advantage over the other. Distance
5 miles. Time 2 hours.

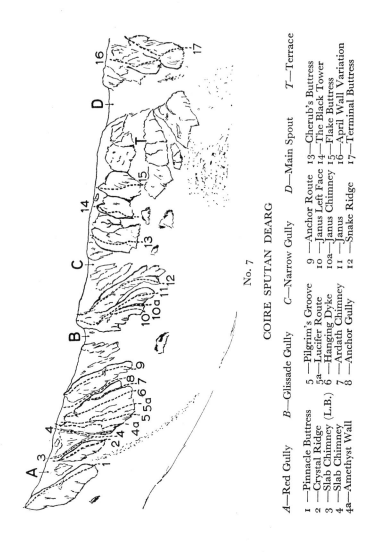

No. 7

COIRE SPUTAN DEARG

A—Red Gully   B—Glissade Gully   C—Narrow Gully   D—Main Spout   T—Terrace

1 —Pinnacle Buttress
2 —Crystal Ridge
3 —Slab Chimney (L.B.)
4 —Slab Chimney
4a—Amethyst Wall
5 —Pilgrim's Groove
5a—Lucifer Route
6 —Hanging Dyke
7 —Ardath Chimney
8 —Anchor Gully
9 —Anchor Route
10 —Janus Left Face
10a—Janus Chimney
11 —Janus
12 —Snake Ridge
13 —Cherub's Buttress
14 —The Black Tower
15 —Flake Buttress
16 —April Wall Variation
17 —Terminal Buttress

2. *From the Hutchison Memorial Hut.* Follow the stream coming down the wide grassy basin to the left of the cliffs of Creagan a' Choire Etchachan and go over the col between that top and Derry Cairngorm. Distance $1\frac{3}{4}$ miles.

CAMPING

Good camping sites exist on the Derry Lodge approach, at the Robber's Copse—a stand of old Caledonian pines at the ford over the Luibeg, 2 miles from Derry Lodge, and further up Glen Luibeg on the raised green shelves at the confluence of the Allt Càrn a' Mhaim on the left bank.

THE BUTTRESSES

With one exception these are narrow and compact, offering little scope for variation. They commence high on the left of the corrie, adjacent to a sweep of polished slabs and extend north in a descending line, merging gradually into broken rock near the low col leading to Loch Etchachan. They are intersected at three points by wide scree gullies (the Red Spouts), which provide easy means of descent in summer. These enable a party to accomplish without trouble many climbs on a single visit.

ROUTES

PINNACLE BUTTRESS 350 feet MODERATE. GRADE 2

First ascent: S. R. Tewnion, J. Tewnion and W. A. Russell   *May 2nd 1948*
First winter ascent: W. D. Brooker and J. W. Morgan
                                           January 5th 1950

The first buttress from the left. It is easily recognised by its having a ledge of easy ground coming in from the right, half-way up. In winter, this looks like a notch.

E

Start up an obvious line of weakness at the foot of the buttress. At 40 feet, scramble up a short stretch to the foot of a long groove forming an angle between the true crest on the right and a 110-foot cracked slab on the left. Start in the groove, but leave it soon to slant up the slab to reach its top left corner. Above this the climb degenerates. The true crest has been climbed (M.S.).

Winter: The lower rocks are usually easy, but the long groove may contain ice. Ice may also cover completely the normally easy upper section. Allow $2\frac{1}{2}$–3 hours.

THE RED GULLY

The gully between Pinnacle Buttress and Crystal Ridge. It is not a summer climb, but the bright red screes which it sends far into the corrie from its disintegrating headwall form a useful landmark in misty weather. In winter, it is little more than a steep snow walk, with sometimes a respectable, but easily passed cornice.

CRYSTAL RIDGE   270 feet   DIFFICULT. GRADE 3

First ascent: R. Still and Miss E. J. Lawrence
September 1st 1948
First winter ascent: W. D. Brooker and M. Smith
January 5th 1949

The climb follows the crest of a great slab, angling into and bolstering up the left flank of Grey Man's Crag, the biggest mass of rock on the face. The slab has a vertical left wall bordering Red Gully. The climbing is continuous, on clean, sound rock throughout. The angle is not excessive, so that added rope lengths may give a false impression of height.

Start at the foot of the ridge and follow moderately-angled rock to the base of the great slab. This gives about

100 feet of good climbing and forms the most difficult pitch—follow the crest as closely as possible on good holds to a belay at the top. An interesting arête leads to a shelf in 70 feet. From the shelf, climb a further pitch on the right side to easy ground.

Winter: The great slab usually carries little snow, but much time may be spent on it clearing ice from holds. The hardest pitch may be the last one. The upper snow-slopes to the cornice of Red Gully are moderately angled beyond a snow-arête which usually forms at the top of the ridge. 400 feet to the cornice.

Grey Man's Crag

This compact mass of foliated slabs and grooves dwarfs its nearest neighbours. It is the biggest buttress on the face. The basal rocks due to prolonged snow-cover are unweathered and form a curious, pink hem to the brown, upper rocks.

Six routes appear on the mass. First from the left is Slab Chimney cutting deeply into its left side. Amethyst Wall goes up the rocks overlooking Slab Chimney. Pilgrim's Groove, Lucifer Route and Hanging Dyke are face routes nearer the centre. For length and continuity the Groove and the Dyke are the best in the corrie. Ardath Chimney is on the right side—short, but defined.

SLAB CHIMNEY   400 feet   DIFFICULT.   GRADE 2

First ascent (winter): A. Parker and J. Young
                                March 17th 1949
First summer ascent: G. H. Leslie and M. Smith; J. Harper
        and G. Davidson   *August 22nd 1954*

This is the most impressive gully in the corrie. Fol-lowing an open start it narrows, then cuts deeply into

Grey Man's Crag. A left branch, almost a corner, goes up the side of Crystal Ridge. The main gully is inconspicuous from the corrie floor but shows up well in winter as the right leg of a perfect Y from the Luibeg approach.

Good rock scenery but wet and vegetated, lacking stances and belays.

The first pitch, an indefinite slab and piled-block scramble, can be avoided by taking to the drier rock of Crystal Ridge. The second starts on a moss-grown wall which leads to a big cave high on the right, but not on the route. Leave the wall for a grooved slab on the right of the watercourse. Halfway up the slab make a long stride to the left across the watercourse (V.D.) and continue up avoiding the water by straddling. The bed apart from an indefinite pitch is easy to the junction. The main gully bends inwards and narrows. 70 feet of moderate climbing leads to an impressive chokestone blocking the gully between high walls. Evade the overhang by a climb on the right wall. Steep vegetation follows to a second chokestone turned on the right after which awkward mossy slabs and more vegetation lead to a point where the gully forks. The right fork—the best finish—is a narrow chimney leading from a loose perch on the right wall to easy rock; the left fork, up a slabby corner, is less interesting.

Winter: The best winter gully in the corrie. Early in the season the three pitches above the branch are iced up and provide hard climbing; later the lower chokestone is built over. The second chokestone and the rocks on its right form the crux. On the first ascent this occupied 2 hours. All pitches may disappear after heavy snow and towards the end of the season.

The left branch, without interest in summer, forms a snow shelf running up the side of Crystal Ridge to the snow-arête at the top of that route (Grade 1). This also was first climbed by the pioneers of the main gully winter ascent.

AMETHYST WALL   400 feet   VERY SEVERE (V.)

First ascent: R. W. P. Barclay and W. D. Brooker
June 10th 1956

Between Slab Chimney and Pilgrim's Groove is a fine steep buttress with a prominent slanting chimney running up its left side to easy ground overlooking Slab Chimney. This hard but rather inelegant route follows the chimney, traverses on to the buttress 100 feet up, leaves the buttress when it becomes overhanging and finally regains it in its upper section.

Climb the slanting chimney-crack to an exit on the left (100 feet). Scramble up 20 feet then traverse down and right on to the smooth face. Work up to the right by three flake cracks and then up an easy gangway to the left (70 feet, S.). The crest overhangs. Slant left up a slab to a grass platform. Go right for 15 feet to a recess under a big overhang. Climb the overhang by swinging up to the right to grasp a flake (combined tactics, V.S.) and follow a vertical crack (30 feet) to a stance. Follow the crest on slabs to the top.

Variation: Above and to the left of the grass platform a remarkable crack can be seen cleaving the face— Plumbline (H.S.). Mantelshelf on to a tiny ledge 10 feet above, then use a very low left handhold to swing across into a groove. Stance 15 feet higher. Climb an overhang, enter the crack and follow it (care required at top). Straddle a chimney (15 feet) and exit to ledge on right. Easy to plateau on cracked slabs. (R. W. P. Barclay and W. D. Brooker, June 10th 1956.)

PILGRIM'S GROOVE   450 feet   VERY SEVERE

First ascent: S. R. Tewnion, J. Tewnion and E. L. Smith
September 18th 1949

Situated just left of centre on the buttress and to the left of the lowest rock. It follows a defined groove developing into a chimney higher up.

Start in the groove at a cairn and climb moderate rock for 150 feet to a chokestone. Gain its top from a mantelshelf on the left wall. Now climb an inset corner immediately on the left (20 feet, crux). It is a delicate problem to snatch a small knob almost out of reach at the top of the corner. Above this the groove is easier to a grass ledge and belay below the continuation chimney. This rises for 60 feet in four steps, each progressively more difficult. Some 15 feet higher there is a belay at the back of a cave. Two chokestones are turned on the left in the next 80 feet and the top of the chimney gained by a moderate rock rib of 120 feet.

LUCIFER ROUTE   450 feet   SEVERE

First ascent: M. Scott, D. Macrae and R. Ellis
October 21st 1956

Start immediately to the right of the Pilgrim's Groove cairn. Take the groove straight ahead for 170 feet to a platform below an overhang (M.). Go up the vertical right wall (V.D.) and then up the groove above the overhang to a large block climbed in the right corner to a grass ledge. Climb to the right over a detached block then up the top left-hand edge of a huge slab to a ledge overlooking Pilgrim's Groove (piton belay). From the ledge enter Pilgrim's Groove by a severe move and follow this route to the top.

HANGING DYKE   400 feet   VERY DIFFICULT

First ascent: A. Parker and J. Young   *March 29th 1949*

This climb, for which two routes were fully described, named and entered as separate climbs in the general Cairngorms Guide 1950, has been proved to be the Original Route of the pioneer party. At the time of the first ascent, snow covered the first and part of the second pitches. The second ascent was made under the impression that the route was still virgin. The party named it Hanging Dyke. With due respect to the pioneers, this name has been adopted. It is the one in customary usage.

The climb follows the backbone of the buttress by the line of a geological dyke throughout. A fine open route —the best for continuity in the corrie. The crux is delicate and exposed.

Start to the right of the lowest rocks at the foot of a broad slab (cairn). The dyke goes up the centre of this slab. Follow the dyke to a small ledge (piton belay), then climb a grass-filled crack to a good stance. Climb a wide slab inclining left, by a series of parallel cracks to a sloping corner. The dyke steepens, forming a rib to the left of a groove. Climb the rib for 60 feet on small holds (crux), until the dyke falls back into a chimney. The continuation of the dyke provides a further 100 feet of interesting climbing until easier ground is reached.

Notes

1. It is possible that the pioneer party followed a line some 20 feet to the right on the second and third pitches.
2. Median Route (C.C.J. 16.289) is identical to the route described.

ARDATH CHIMNEY   150 feet   DIFFICULT. GRADE 3

First ascent: J. Tewnion and M. Smith   *May 20th 1950*
First winter ascent: J. Y. L. Hay   *April 2nd 1955*

The right wall of Grey Man's Crag falls into Anchor Gully. As one rounds the corner of the buttress to the screes of the gully a conspicuous chimney will be seen cleaving this wall. This is Ardath Chimney, straight-cut for 150 feet, thereafter falling back into a grassy depression.

Climb the initial chokestone on the left. Piled blocks follow to a thread belay round a small chokestone. Above rises the smooth water-worn chimney bed. Climb this by backing up for 20 feet before making an awkward step to the right to reach a belay. Small pitches may be found on the right to the plateau.

Winter: A confined route, steep and sporting. The ultimate 20 feet in the chimney is usually a good ice-pitch. Better early in the season when there is ice above the first chokestone. First ascent under poor thaw conditions. 350 feet to plateau.

ANCHOR GULLY   300 feet   MODERATE. GRADE 1

First ascent: I. M. Brooker, A. E. Anton and G. Mathieson
May 16th 1948

The gully between Grey Man's Crag and Anchor Route. So named from the formation of snow at its foot. The first winter party is unknown.

The gully starts with an easy chokestone passed on the left. 20 feet higher, climb a short wall by the right hand of two grooves over a short overhang. Another easy chokestone follows, above which there are only indefinite pitches.

Winter: There may be a pitch early in the season, at the neck low in the gully. Later the gully becomes quite straightforward except for the cornice which can usually be outflanked on the right.

ANCHOR ROUTE   400 feet   DIFFICULT. GRADE 3

First ascent: W. D. Brooker, C. Hutcheon and D. A.
    Sutherland   *June 26th 1949*
First winter ascent: G. Adams and R. W. P. Barclay
                                     December 25th 1955

The route lies on the double-tiered buttress bordering Anchor Gully on its right. The lower tier serves as an introduction to the upper, which is more interesting— 300 feet of good climbing. The left edge overlooking the gully is followed.

Go up an attractive groove on the lowest rocks, then scramble to the terrace below left edge of upper tier. Start on this by a crack on a slab (cairn) and follow the edge to a steep slabby section, turned by a short, steep chimney on the gully wall. Avoid an overhang higher up on the right. The buttress now develops into twin arêtes, the left-hand giving the best finish.

Winter: The lower tier is often well snowed up and inconsequential; the upper tier is best gained from Anchor Gully. The ordinary summer route has not been followed. On the only ascent recorded (under heavy powder) a diagonal rightward course was taken from near the summer start, finishing alongside the right edge of the rightmost arête. A piton was used to safeguard last move. Time: 2½ hours.

THE NEXT SECTION OF CLIFF to the right (north) of Anchor Route, comprising two long ridges, lies between two scree gullies. The wider is Glissade Gully; the narrower and rightmost separates the ridges from three small buttresses, compact, close-set, lying high under the plateau and facing down the Luibeg. North of these again, past a sheet of slab descending low into the corrie, is the main Red Spout, a wide gravelly corridor beyond which rises the final buttress.

GLISSADE GULLY

Set near the centre of the cliffs this is the natural highway summer and winter between plateau and corrie floor. In summer it is scree filled, in winter steep enough to give good, safe glissading. The left wall is a small broken buttress which has been climbed in winter in avalanche conditions (J. Tewnion and G. Dey, February 1951).

JANUS   450 feet   DIFFICULT

First ascent: K. Winram and M. Smith: E. L. Smith and
     J. Tewnion   *May 22nd 1949*

The left-hand of the twin ridges beyond Glissade Gully. It has two sections; a lower, cleft by Janus Chimney into two faces and an upper, a steep buttress with a notched terminating ridge.

Start up a groove at the lowest rocks (cairn) and follow the rib on the right of Janus Chimney. Above an easy middle section, climb the upper buttress on the left side above Glissade Gully by going round a ledge to the left past an initial groove. When the ledge peters out, bear sharp right up a second groove to the crest. An exposed pitch (crux).

JANUS: LEFT FACE   200 feet   VERY SEVERE

First ascent: J. Y. L. Hay, A. O'F. Will, J. Ross, C. Martin
and G. Adams   *April 12th 1956*

An enjoyable variant up the steep rib on the left of
Janus Chimney. One piton for direct aid.

Climb groove from foot of rib to platform then move
right to crest. Swing up left on steep rock using flake to
main platform. Climb shallow depression above to foot
of vertical crack with an overhung top. Use layback and
traverse right to crest using a piton. Follow ridge to
easy ground below upper buttress.

JANUS CHIMNEY   150 feet   VERY DIFFICULT

First ascent: E. L. Smith, T. Shaw and A. Cameron
                                          July 1st 1950

The conspicuous cleft in Janus' lower section. Climb
the initial chokestone on the left. Two mossy blocks
followed by loose vegetation lead to a small cave. It is a
hard move getting round the chokestone above. Solve
the problem by backing up (thread belay). Easy to
upper buttress.

SNAKE RIDGE   450 feet   HARD SEVERE

First ascent: W. D. Brooker, D. A. Sutherland and C.
Hutcheon   *June 25th 1949*

The second of the long ridges to the right of Glissade
Gully, so named from its fancied resemblance as seen
from the top, to a snake, head down. For easier recog-
nition its lower rocks fan out into three ridges giving a
fair impression of inverted Prince of Wales' feathers. The
left side of the ridge is high and overhanging, the right

is low and angles easily into a grass rake running along-side.

Start on the left feather and follow the crest which soon becomes a smooth knife-edge leading to the top of the snake's head. For another 50 feet the crest is sharp to a platform (cairn). Above this is a step in the ridge. Climb this by following the left edge of the wall to slabs and a belay (60 feet). The crux follows. Use combined tactics to surmount a short wall on the left and from a stance on a flake go up a holdless 8-foot groove to the crest (H.S.). Good climbing for another 100 feet leads to the broken upper buttress.

THE COMPACT BUTTRESSES forming a close-set trio to the right of Snake Ridge and separated from it by the narrow scree-gully are named from left to right: Cherub's Buttress, The Black Tower and Flake Buttress. Although relatively short they give interesting climbs on rock of steeper angle than is generally met with on the other buttresses. They are separated from each other by wet, slabby depressions which become ice-falls in winter; the left-hand being the more formidable. These are un-climbed.

CHERUB'S BUTTRESS   300 feet   DIFFICULT

First ascent: J. Tewnion and A. Alexander: E. L. Smith
    and M. Smith   *July 3rd 1949*

The buttress is in two sections; a lower, main section ending in a pinnacle, and above some easy ground, an upper ring of cliff forming a small amphitheatre. The lower section is a grand, unbroken wall with an intro-ductory rib leading to its right-hand edge. To the right of the rib there is a grass depression, beyond which, an offshoot flying ridge supports the upperworks of the buttress. The crux is exposed and requires a delicate movement.

Start up a sporting flake crack then an interesting slab until the way is barred at 80 feet by a vertical nose. Move into the depression on the right to a belay. Traverse left onto the exposed wall and climb into a groove with sketchy handholds (crux—V.D.). Piled blocks lead to a belay. A chimney and an arête follow for 100 feet to the amphitheatre. From a cairn, go up under an overhang and traverse right into a chimney, then left to the plateau by slabs and a second chimney.

THE BLACK TOWER   270 feet   SEVERE

First ascent: T. W. Patey, G. B. Leslie and J. M. Taylor
April 21st 1952

The central and hardest of the trio. The climb though short is excellent and has great character. The form of the buttress changes when seen from different angles. From the corrie floor it is squat and compact; its finer and truer form is best seen from Cherub's Buttress from where it appears as a tapering, twisted spire having a curious, square summital-block reminiscent of the greater Aiguilles.

Start on the left about 50 feet above the lowest rock, in a slabby amphitheatre which, strewn with saxifrages, is almost a rock-garden. Follow a groove developing into a narrow chimney for 80 feet to easier ground. Climb broken slabs for 30 feet on the left to a platform at the foot of a steep 20-foot groove on the edge of the tower. Enter the groove from the right by a severe move and climb it to a platform and block. Round a corner to the left, climb a steep slab by a 20-foot crack to a short arête. Thence, by a delicate traverse across a slab on the right it is possible to regain the crest and summit of the tower by a short steep crack. The tower is linked to the plateau by a broken arête.

FLAKE BUTTRESS   300 feet   MODERATE. GRADE 3

First ascent: J. Tewnion and E. L. Smith: K. Winram and
    M. Smith   *May 22nd 1949*
First winter ascent: W. D. Brooker and S. McPherson
                                                April 10th 1950

The most symmetrical of the trio, being ridge-like in form. An excellent route and popular. It has a splendid variety of pitches nowhere more than difficult. Hard variations have been made on the lower section.

A chimney slightly right of centre provides a good start (cairn) and leads to an awkward slab on the right. Easy to a stance on the broken crest. Tackle the next pitch by starting on the right, then work back left horizontally by a crack to a right-angled corner with a sloping floor. There is a good hold above for a swing-out. Head left to a stance on the crest. Go up a chimney on the right and then by easy ledges gain a fine pulpit stance behind a huge flake. Climb the vertical crack immediately in front on grand holds and continue up slabs to a gap. The gap looks loose but is quite firm. Across the gap the climb finishes, but ignore the easy ground and take the arête ahead over two man-traps.

Winter: Deep, powder snow on the lower part of the climb proved to be the main difficulty on the first ascent. The upper buttress held less snow and went easily. No times recorded.

NORTH OF FLAKE BUTTRESS, extending low into the corrie is a sweep of smooth slab cut by a terrace which provides a useful means of access to the Main Spout and its attendant buttresses on the right.

THE MAIN SPOUT

This, the widest of the spouts, is a walk summer and winter. Terminal Buttress and April Wall Variation are climbs on its lower, right flank. A series of small buttresses continues to the plateau on this flank. These may give short climbs of the 100-120 foot order.

TERMINAL BUTTRESS   230 feet   MILD SEVERE

First ascent: J. Tewnion, E. L. Smith and M. Smith
September 11th 1949

The last of the buttresses and the biggest mass on the right side of the Main Spout. It is seen to its best advantage "en face", when the crux appears as an impressive crescent-shaped groove on its right flank.

A minor gully runs up the right side. Start in this gully at the foot of the right wall. Climb wrinkled and puckered rock for a steep initial 40 feet; a few feet higher traverse left round a rib and move up over an awkward projecting spur to a deep V groove and a belay on the edge of the gully. The groove steepens and 20 feet of hard climbing leads to an overhang. Move left round this and continue up the groove for 15 feet until forced out horizontally to the left and round a corner to a stance. There is a choice of routes for the next 40 feet to a broad ledge sloping right. Climb the wall above by a shattered rib 15 feet along the ledge and finish by a short moderate pitch.

APRIL WALL VARIATION   150 feet   SEVERE

First ascent: G. B. Leslie, T. W. Patey and J. M. Taylor
April 21st 1952

This is a variation in name only. It is actually a follow-on from the previous route described on to the side-wall of the buttress higher up the Main Spout and provides an exhilarating continuation of the Terminal Buttress climb.

From the broad shelf or ledge sloping right at the top of Terminal, traverse left to a steep wall and start up the nearest rocks until forced well to the left on to the main section of the wall. After 80 feet, a small ledge with a belay is reached in an exposed situation. Make a sensational move on good holds to the left and still slanting left, a severe mantleshelf movement followed by an airy corner, leads to a shallow gully in about 50 feet. This is topped by a short, easy chimney.

COIRE AN LOCHAN UAINE

This lies south of Coire Sputan Dearg. On the O.S. maps (1″ and 6″) it is treated as part of that corrie and is unnamed.

Its only climbing interest is in winter when its rim is often heavily corniced. The best climb is a direct ascent to the Stob Coire Sputan Dearg (4095 feet) from the loch, by steep open slopes, finishing by a narrow gully to the right of the Stob (c. 1000 feet)—a most beautiful, satisfying and direct approach to Ben Macdhui.

THE CRAGS OF COIRE ETCHACHAN
AND LOCH ETCHACHAN

MANY rock climbers in the past must have used the path to Ben Macdhui and the Shelter Stone which climbs through the defile of Coire Etchachan, yet the grand crag flanking the left side of the corrie remained untouched until 1949—last but one of the great Cairngorm faces to be explored. The most accessible of cliffs; steep, defined buttresses; forbidding overhangs and slabs—the neglect could not have been due to a contempt occasioned by familiarity, the more likely cause was the dismissal of the rocks in an earlier guide as being "rather fragmentary". There is no Cairngorm cliff with less talus!

This cliff is on Creagan a' Choire Etchachan (3629 feet), an eastern top of Ben Macdhui. The smaller crags and long rock-spines on the north side of the corrie are on Stob Coire Etchachan, the 3551-foot top of Beinn Mheadhoin, and it is this face which, dominating the head of Glen Derry, does much to enliven the monotony of that glen's upper part.

The crags of Loch Etchachan are indefinite and provide poor summer climbing. Fair sport, however, can be had under snow, but their greatest value lies in their perfecting a winter landscape which in point of simple grandeur, spaciousness and air of serenity is peerless among our mountains.

The Hutchison Memorial Hut: This open shelter built in 1954 in Coire Etchachan near the 2250 foot contour is an ideally-situated base, amidst wonderful scenery, from which the climbs may be made. The main crag is only 20 minutes distant.

APPROACHES

1. *From Derry Lodge* by Glen Derry and the path to Ben
   Macdhui—4½ miles to the hut. Time: 1 hour 40
   minutes.
2. *From the Shelter Stone* by the track over the Beinn
   Mheadhoin–Cairn Etchachan col to the outflow of
   Loch Etchachan and descent to the hut. Time: 1 hour

THE CREAGAN A' CHOIRE
ETCHACHAN FACE

The main climbing theatre—a straight line of cliff
averaging 400 feet in height, situated high on the left
skyline. It comprises three buttresses, three gullies, a
remarkable ascending line of overhangs and a formidable
downsweep of high-angled slabs.

On the left the face is dominated by The Bastion, the
largest buttress. This is demarcated on its left by Forked
Gully which separates the main face from a line of small
crags. The right flank of The Bastion drops in un-
relieved verticality for 300 feet into a dark couloir—The
Corridor. The right wall of this recess is formed by
Juniper Buttress split by a central depression or chimney
into two ribs. Beyond these Square-Cut Gully separates
Juniper from Pioneer Buttress. From the base of this
buttress overhangs rise in undercut steps poised over
two prominent grassy scoops. The crag is then severed
by the Red Chimney. Finally on the right the great
expanse of the smooth glistening Crimson Slabs merges
into more broken rock above the track in the corrie.

The rock is typical granite, varying in formation,
character and adhesive quality over the whole face. Its
overall soundness is marred by dubious patches at two
points only—in Avalanche Gully and The Corridor.

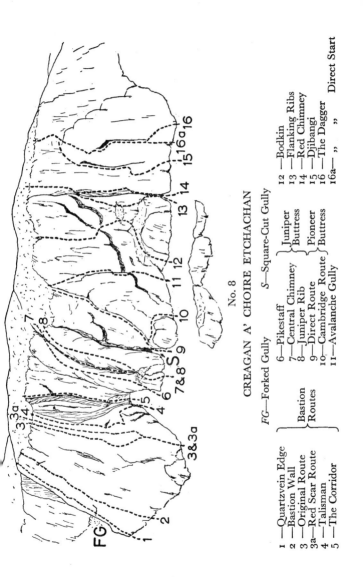

No. 8

CREAGAN A' CHOIRE ETCHACHAN

FG—Forked Gully   S—Square-Cut Gully

1 —Quartzvein Edge
2 —Bastion Wall } Bastion Routes
3 —Original Route } Bastion Routes
3a —Red Scar Route
4 —Talisman
5 —The Corridor

6 —Pikestaff
7 —Central Chimney } Juniper Buttress
8 —Juniper Rib } Juniper Buttress
9 —Direct Route
10 —Cambridge Route } Pioneer Buttress
11 —Avalanche Gully

12 —Bodkin
13 —Flanking Ribs
14 —Red Chimney
15 —Djibangi
16 —The Dagger
16a— ,, ,, Direct Start

The roughest rock will be found on The Bastion and Juniper Buttress. Vegetation is chiefly confined to the central sector, the least interesting part of the face.

The climbs left to right:

FORKED GULLY   300 feet   GRADE 1

Not a rock climb, but a useful means of descent. Care is required because of loose vegetation overlying slabs. It gives an easy climb in winter when built up fully. The right branch is the more sporting exit. A good glissade.

The Bastion

This, the largest buttress, presents a broad, wedge-shaped base to the corrie. It is steepest on its right edge which forms a remarkable gable of smooth granite. Five routes go up the mass: Quartzvein Edge and Bastion Wall on the left and Original Route, Red Scar Route and The Talisman on the right. Between, there is a sweep of grooved and cracked slabs with no definite features, offering scope for variation.

QUARTZVEIN EDGE 400 feet MODERATE. GRADE 3

First ascent: K. Winram, G. C. Greig and M. Smith
June 15th 1952
First winter ascent: J. Y. L. Hay, G. Adams and A. Thom
December 29th 1956

A popular climb following the left edge of the Bastion overlooking Forked Gully. Good, rough rock and adequate belays.

Start at the foot of Forked Gully beyond a detached

block (cairn). Climb a 10-foot wall with a piece of quartz inset, then follow the edge on good rock for 120 feet to a gravel patch. Climb a groove slanting left by laybacking up a crack—slabs complete the pitch. Go up more cracked slabs to the lower of two shelves. Make a right traverse up to the higher shelf at the site of some quartz intrusions. The shelf develops into an open chimney ending in a pile of jumbled blocks poised over the gully. A scree funnel to the top. More difficult finishes can be had on the false tower on the right of the open chimney.

Winter: A worth-while climb with sustained difficulty under hard snow. The first party finished up the right wall of the false tower. This was the crux. Time: 3½ hours.

BASTION WALL   400 feet   DIFFICULT

First ascent: W. Kelly and P. Leys   *May 31st 1953*

On the left section of the buttress, approaching Quartzvein Edge at mid-height then diverging. A route of uniform steepness and difficulty. Mainly slab climbing interrupted by grass ledges with few belays. It is open to considerable variation.

Start 200 feet below Forked Gully at a small grass shelf (cairn). High up on the left is a curious, perched block; the route passes some 40 feet to its right. For 200 feet follow the line of least resistance up slabs with grassy ledges, trending leftwards to a point where easy ground leads to the gravel patch of Quartzvein Edge. Here, however, diverge well to the right up steep rock initially, then by indeterminate climbing to the top.

ORIGINAL ROUTE   450 feet   MILD SEVERE

First ascent: D. A. Sutherland and K. Winram
                                              April 1st 1950

A good climb with continuous difficulty over many interesting pitches.

Start to the right of the lowest rock on the right of the buttress and slant left up an easy depression ending at an overhanging wall 150 feet up. (This point may be reached by an easy traverse from the foot of the Corridor.) A fine slab pitch round the corner of the wall on the left leads to a 7-foot pedestal. A clean wall-pitch (50 feet, V.D.) a few feet to the right follows. The side of a vertical rib is climbed and a short chimney gained by a delicate stride (S.) to the right. Above is a large platform. From this, climb the left-hand of two chimneys 8 feet apart for 12 feet and move right at the top. On the left, sloping ledges (V.D.) give access to a long V groove leading to easy ground.

RED SCAR ROUTE   450 feet   SEVERE

First ascent: T. W. Patey and W. D. Brooker
                                              October 25th 1953

Follows a line fairly close to the right edge of the Bastion. A red vein of unweathered granite is evident near the acute edge of the buttress; the route touches this at one point. In its last 150 feet it is close to and parallel with the Original Route.

Start in the depression of Original Route but as soon as possible veer upwards to the right. Climb a short, vegetated wall to reach the foot of a small rock spur. Go up this by a 12-foot slab on the right to a chimney of red rock. Climb the chimney (12 feet, crux) and traverse left for 20 feet and climb another chimney, narrow with a stance at the top. Following a short slab traverse, continue on a line slightly rightward for 60 feet, finishing with an awkward 10-foot wall. The last 150 feet offers a choice of routes.

THE TALISMAN   300 feet   HARD SEVERE (V.)

First ascent: W. D. Brooker and K. A. Grassick
June 24th 1956

The best route in the corrie. Follows the defined right edge of the Bastion on the brink of the Corridor. Steep, clean with continuous difficulty.

Start from a platform between two huge blocks against the wall about 20 feet up the Corridor. Climb crack behind the block to a ledge at 40 feet. Move right and climb huge slab on good holds to piton belay at 40 feet. Traverse left for 50 feet to a stand with poor belay on the crest (delicate, M.S.). Detour left round an overhang and climb crest to a flake in a corner. Move left to a groove and up to a piton belay under an overhanging corner (70 feet, S.). Climb the corner to an excellent stance (H.S.). The crest is now easy for 30 feet and one could escape to the left, but the following 120 feet ahead gives continuously hard climbing on the slabby crest sometimes using holds on the sheer right wall.

THE broad couloir shadowed by the vertical gable of the Bastion and hemmed in by that uncompromising wall and the incised flank of Juniper Buttress is "The Corridor". It would appear to offer a not too difficult climb to the plateau but actually its final crack has not been climbed directly. Being rather grimy it is best suited as a winter climb; nevertheless in dry conditions it is worth doing for the sake of its top pitch:

THE CORRIDOR   350 feet   GRADE 3–4

Direct Line: VERY SEVERE; Alternative Finish: SEVERE
First ascent (winter): F. R. Malcolm and A. Thom
March 20th 1954
First ascent (summer) by Alternative Finish: J. Y. L. Hay,
    A. P. Crichton and W. Christie   *July 21st 1955*
First ascent (summer) by Direct Line: T. W. Patey and A.
    Duguid   *August 15th 1955*

In the lower part a 120-foot pointed slab leads to a
dirty runnel. Beyond this some chokestones are passed
easily but the next pitch over some large jammed blocks
is more difficult. Steep scree then leads to the back of a
huge cave below the unclimbed crack. Starting 12 feet
above the last substantial platform, make a 25-foot
horizontal traverse across the slab on the right (delicate
on minute holds, V.S.). Once the edge is gained a steep
step is avoided on the right and a good stance gained at
the top. Slant left to finish at the top of the corner crack.

Alternative Finish. Move right from below the large
jammed blocks and descend to a grass terrace. Start
climbing the rib by a narrow crack and continue to a
large boss, then go up slabs and a groove to belay
(100-foot run-out, S.). Finish as before.

Winter: Variable but often providing a hard climb
early in the season or after thaw. On the first ascent the
main difficulty lay in the final ice-wall above the great
cave. This is the unclimbed summer pitch and at that
time presented an ice-bulge 30 feet high. From an
excellent stance the party traversed right from the cave
and overcame the obstacle after fixing two ice-pitons.
To maintain balance while cutting another was used as
an ice-claw for the left hand ($1\frac{1}{4}$ hours). The jammed
blocks pitch was banked with snow allowing direct
access to the great cave. Total time: $3\frac{3}{4}$ hours.

Juniper Buttress

Between the Corridor and Square-Cut Gully. Above its steep lower 150 feet a grassy section intervenes. The buttress is split by the Central Chimney into two ribs. That on the left is Pikestaff; the right is Juniper Rib.

PIKESTAFF   350 feet   SEVERE

First ascent: T. W. Patey, W. D. Brooker and J. Y. L. Hay   *August 7th 1954*

A steep route on clean rock but escapes are possible into Central Chimney below the final two, hard pitches.

Go up the Corridor flank of the rib to a point just beyond a ferny trough which climbs to the grass section of the buttress. Start beside a curious little pocket in the rock. Climb two short walls and then up alongside the trough to within 15 feet of its top. Slant up the Corridor wall for 60 feet by steep cracks until a break on the right leads to the crest. Follow the rib directly ahead. First comes a smooth nose (V.D.), then easier rock to a pointed belay. Take off from a flake on the left (S.) and finish the pitch by moving right. The final 80-foot pitch follows (V.D.).

JUNIPER RIB   350 feet   DIFFICULT

First ascent: I. M. Brooker and Miss M. Newbigging
                                                 July 6th 1950

Originally named Juniper Buttress by first party (C.C.J. 16.227). Good rock especially in the lower section.

Start from the lowest rocks of the buttress and climb to an obvious V cleft. The ascent of this (D.) gives access

to the grassy section (other variations have been made
on this lower part). The natural line from here is up
Central Chimney but move right on to the rib and climb
a series of difficult pitches separated by ledges to easier
scrambling at the top.

CENTRAL CHIMNEY 350 feet MODERATE. GRADE 3

First ascent: Uncertain
First winter ascent: T. W. Patey, A. O'F. Will, G. Adams
    and M. Smith   *February 27th 1955*

The chimney separating the ribs—gained by the V
cleft of the former route. It offers nothing more than
moderate climbing over indefinite pitches above the
cleft in summer.

Winter: First ascent after blizzards, on deep uncon-
solidated snow, required care, for on only one pitch (a
deviation on to Pikestaff above the summer grass slope)
could the party climb on rock. Ice was present in the
initial cleft and in the narrow chimney above the deviation. A beautiful finish up the snow apron (often well
corniced and liable to avalanche) above Juniper Rib.
Time: $2\frac{1}{2}$ hours.

Square-Cut Gully

A slabby trench between Juniper and Pioneer buttresses ending in overhangs half-way up, extensions of
the wall of Juniper Rib. Although uninspiring in
summer, in winter it contains ice, and that in quantity;
in particular one magnificent ice-pillar at the overhangs.

Direct ascent in summer appears problematical.
Curious parties have been diverted on to Pioneer
Buttress where the general line followed is that of the
Winter Route.

WINTER ROUTE   350 feet   GRADE 3

First ascent: W. D. Brooker, J. W. Morgan and D. A.
    Sutherland   *January 2nd 1950*

The party started in Square-Cut Gully but below its
first major ice-pitch they traversed on to Pioneer Buttress
on the right. The rib of the buttress was followed for
some distance then a left traverse was made and a 50-foot
ice-pitch encountered near the top (5 hours).

The general line of this route (with variations) has
been followed in summer by many parties. It is rather
artificial and unsatisfactory (first ascent: J. Gadd and
Mrs Gadd, July 1955).

Pioneer Buttress

The opening route on the cliff was made here by a
C.U.M.C. party in March 1949. They named it the
"Grandes Jorasses" to whose north face the main cliff
bears a strong family resemblance under snow. This
name, alas, would have been a rather startling departure
from (at that time) a traditionally staid Cairngorm
nomenclature—the party settled for Pioneer Route.
This in turn has given way to Cambridge Route, and the
whole buttress was named Pioneer Buttress.

In appearance it takes the form of a short-based right-
angled triangle, the hypotenuse being its easier-angled
left edge bordering Square-Cut Gully. From its bottom
right edge a line of overhangs rears up to the plateau in
progressive steps.

CAMBRIDGE ROUTE   350 feet   SEVERE

First ascent: A. Parker and J. Young   *March 26th 1949*

A route following a not very obvious line starting on
the right flank, and at 80 feet traversing the entire

buttress to its easier, left edge. This point can be attained
by easy pitches direct from the foot of Square-Cut Gully.
The subsequent climbing is nowhere more than difficult.

Start 30 feet up from, and to the left of the lowest rock.
A deceptive, innocent-looking slab is overcome by a
crack in the left corner (S.). Above, a large groove slants
upwards to the left. Follow this for 30 feet to the foot of
a short wall. (Here the pioneers were persuaded by the
appearance of the continuation of the groove to commence their long, leftward traverse.) Step out to an
exposed nose and move up to a little grass ledge. From
here make a delicate step down and traverse across the
bottom of a short slab (S.) to a cramped corner, following
which a short chimney leads to easier rocks on the left
edge of the buttress. Climb up the edge over broken
rocks which merge into a rib higher up. This is climbed
direct, but some manoeuvring is needed near the top.

DIRECT ROUTE   350 feet   DIFFICULT

The route following the entire left edge from the
corner of Square-Cut Gully. Easy pitches lead to the
point where the traverse of the Cambridge Route
finishes on the edge.

———

FROM the foot of Pioneer Buttress to the upper reaches
of the Red Chimney the great overhangs rise in undercut
steps. Avalanche Gully is the steep, narrow fault
breaching the lowest tier and distinguished by the giant
scar of a recent rock-fall in its upper part.

AVALANCHE GULLY   350 feet   VERY SEVERE

First ascent: J. Gadd and Mrs Gadd   *July 1955*

Acting on an entry in the Derry Lodge visitors book which seemed to indicate a definite ascent, the route was investigated and was found to be both hard and dangerous on account of wet rock and loose debris. Not recommended.

The gully is blocked at 150 feet by the overhangs. The impasse is turned by 80 feet of steep climbing on the left of the bed, returning by a very thin traverse higher up. Above this it is continuously difficult and unjustifiable in its looseness.

Two large grass scoops are situated between AVALANCHE GULLY and the RED CHIMNEY. Above them the overhangs menace. From the extreme left of the upper scoop BODKIN slants leftward to breach the overhangs, then goes straight up.

BODKIN   350 feet   SEVERE

First ascent: T. W. Patey, W. W. Hutchison and A. Watson   *July 9th 1954*

Scramble by easy terraces to the upper scoop (150 feet). From the left end slant left to reach a groove beyond which a slab is poised over space. Cross the slab at its lower end on an ascending line of tiny footholds (delicate), and climb the rib at the far side to a stance and belay. A short, upward move and a right traverse lead to a 40-foot groove. Climb this and a short awkward move above to a large recess. Go up the cracked wall on the right. Scrambling.

THE RED CHIMNEY   350 feet   HARD SEVERE
GRADE 4

First ascent: J. Gadd and Mrs Gadd   *July 1955*
First winter ascent: J. Y. L. Hay and R. Ibbotson
February 1959

The prominent rift splitting the cliff on the left of the Crimson Slabs. Normally rather wet, but providing an excellent climb in dry conditions on polished rock with few positive holds. Delicate.

The final part of the chimney, which overhangs and is apparently always wet, is unclimbed. Here Flanking Ribs route (M.S.) is followed to the plateau.

Straddle the initial chimney up to the top overhang and make an awkward exit on the right. Climb unrelenting rock with downward dipping footholds to below the next steep pitch where one pulls out on to the edge on the left to a pointed belay. Return by a fine slab pitch into the chimney and continue up easier rock to a fork. The left branch is easier—a short watered groove. Above this Flanking Ribs route crosses the chimney. The climb can thus be finished by this route up the right bounding rib.

Winter: One ascent recorded. The lower section is often filled with a cascade of clear ice overflowing on to the sleek slabs on the right. The upper chimney is normally choked by a series of vertical ice-bosses and remains unclimbed. The start was by the right-angled grooves to the right of the chimney. The second pitch was the crux—an iced slab with a very delicate left traverse and V.S. at the top. Above this came two ice-pitches with a deviation between on to the rib on the left. A further 70 feet of snow and a 50-foot ice-pitch led to the base of the upper chimney where the Flanking Ribs route was used to the top. Time: $6\frac{1}{2}$ hours.

FLANKING RIBS   350 feet   MILD SEVERE

First ascent: W. D. Brooker and D. A. Sutherland
March 26th 1950

Uses the Red Chimney in its first 50 feet, then goes up the ribs on the left, finally crossing the chimney below its steep 150-foot unclimbed section to continue on a narrow rib on the right.

Go 50 feet up the Red Chimney then climb the left wall to a platform. Avoid a steep wall above by moving left, then go up for 60 feet to a belay. Better still, start some 50 or 60 feet left of Red Chimney and climb 20 feet up the left-hand of two grooves, cross to the other and follow it out. Thence by slabs and walls to the afore-mentioned belay. Continue up another 80-foot wall to a belay (flake). Step left and follow an ill-defined rib up slabs and heathered cracks of continuous difficulty trending right at the top. The line of overhangs looms above. Now cross the chimney to the steep narrow rib on the far side. Follow the rib until a small tower rears up. The crux follows. Ascend to a square recess and from this climb a groove on to a sloping roof. A mossy crack leads to easier rock. Scrambling.

The Crimson Slabs

The finest single feature of the crag—a spectacular sweep of slab 250 feet in breadth and 350 feet in height rising to the right of Red Chimney and set at the extreme angle for rock of such smoothness. It rises unbroken except for two great "dièdres"—the only lines of weakness. The leftmost "dièdre" is Djibangi, the right is The Dagger.

THE DAGGER   350 feet   VERY SEVERE (V.)

First ascent: T. W. Patey and J. Y. L. Hay

September 4th 1955

One of the hardest routes in the massif; very strenuous and sustained. The "dièdre" goes straight up for over 100 feet and culminates in a forbidding overhang. Above this easier grooves lead to the topmost slabs. Pitons are used, more for safeguard than direct aid, though they serve for both.

Steep scrambling and an awkward traverse from the right lead to the foot of the "dièdre" 80 feet up. This is an inch by inch struggle throughout. For the first 20 feet the corner crack admits a leg. Then for 20 feet the groove is grass-choked and slightly harder. In the next section the crack is clean and admits only fingers and toes and two pitons are used in a crack on the right wall (crux). More hard climbing (V.S.) up to a perfect belay but poor stance below the overhang. Surmount the overhang by an awkward move round the bulge and step left (piton, S.). Regain the grass groove above the overhang and continue upwards without difficulty, or traverse left at an obvious ledge and climb a similar easy groove further to the left. These lines converge on a good platform below the last slab where a descending ledge goes down to the right. Climb the slab by a mossy crack slanting right (M.S.). The last pitch then goes straight up on the left on good holds.

Direct Start: Start at grassy alcove at foot of Djibangi beside an obvious right-angled corner. Ascend obliquely to the right for 30 feet beyond a shallow groove. Step left into groove at mid-height and follow to top. Escape to right and climb easily to large ledge at foot of main "dièdre" (H.S.—J. Y. L. Hay and G. Adams).

DJIBANGI   350 feet   VERY SEVERE (V.

First ascent: J. Y. L. Hay, R. Wiseman and A. Cowie
July 22nd 1956

The left-hand "dièdre". A better climb than the Dagger but not so hard. One piton for direct aid. Start at the grassy alcove beneath the "dièdre" and follow a diagonal crack leftwards to a large platform overlooking Red Chimney. Trend right and climb a small corner set in the middle of the slab to a stance in the "dièdre" 90 feet above the platform. Work up the corner to the overhang then continue up the corner (piton) to a stance on the rib on the right (120 feet of hard, continuous climbing). Ascend easy, grassy grooves to the upper slab and final pitches of the Dagger.

THE LESSER CRAGS OF STOB COIRE ETCHACHAN

This top of Beinn Mheadhoin as seen from the lower corrie has a high wedge-shaped face. Long broken ribs with small attendant buttresses are the main feature on the right running up to the pointed summit. The best of the many small buttresses (up to 120 feet) have been climbed (earliest records 1946) and give interesting pitches but they are too short for inclusion. The longest of the ribs gives a moderate scramble but they are of slight value in summer. The face, however, assumes an alpine aspect in winter; then the ribs and open gullies make for sporting, direct routes to the summit of Beinn Mheadhoin from Derry Lodge.

On the left of the centre line from the summit the rocks become more massive and the buttresses form a frieze to the skyline, extending in a descending line to

G

the throat of the corrie. Several courses are found on these of which the more important are:

STAG BUTTRESS   180 feet   VERY DIFFICULT

First ascent: A. Murray, A. Imray and J. McLeod
August 15th 1953

The attractive steep rib forming the lowest rocks at the head of the corrie and skylined as seen from the hut.

Start from the lowest rock or by a chimney-crack on the left (both starts awkward), following which steep ribbed slabs lead to a fine ledge and belay. Traverse left and go up the left edge on steep rock with grand holds until confronted by a steep wall. This can be climbed directly if one is tall, otherwise move right then back left to finish by steep slabs.

SUNDAY CRACK   150 feet   DIFFICULT

First ascent: H. S. M. Bates, T. Shaw, W. W. Hutchison and A. Q. Gardiner   *May 1953*

A crack set into a corner of slabs to the left of Stag Buttress. Scramble 25 feet to a shelf below the crack in the corner (unclimbed) then traverse over steep slabs on the left by a system of cracks to a fault with an overhang. Climb the overhang (awkward) and return to the continuation of the corner crack and follow out.

AMPHITHEATRE EDGE   180 feet   VERY DIFFICULT

First ascent: G. C. Greig and G. H. Leslie   *April 4th 1954*

On the rocks higher and to the right of Stag Buttress and beyond a slanting gully. It forms a prominent edge and becomes well defined higher up.

In the upper section climb a steep tower on the right starting from a comfortable platform. The initial move is strenuous. An awkward mantelshelf 30 feet higher leads to a smooth slab.

BELLFLOWER BUTTRESS 300 feet DIFFICULT

First ascent: K. Winram, G. C. Greig and M. Smith
August 19th 1952

The biggest mass of rock on the face; situated higher and to the right of the previous climbs, almost opposite the door of the hut. "Go as you please" climbing.

The best start is near the centre up an obvious and deceptively difficult heathery chimney with an overhung exit, or by the rocks on its right. Ledges and walls follow. Trend left to a good slab pitch under an overhang higher up. Thereafter go up a steep nose to easy rock.

THE CRAGS ABOVE LOCH ETCHACHAN

The rocks here are either too short or discontinuous to give good climbs. The small isolated buttress on the south side of the loch has been scrambled on and gives short steep problems up to 80-90 feet. The only climb of respectable length is on the east-facing crag of Cairn Etchachan, the 3673-foot top of Ben Macdhui.

LOCHSIDE CHIMNEY 300 feet DIFFICULT

First ascent: M. Scott and R. Ellis *September 1955*

The slanting chimney set in centre of the main crag. Rather artificial. Take every pitch direct ignoring the easy ground on the right in the lower section.

Winter: Under snow should give a sporting climb.

To the right of the main mass is a short, deep, gully which has been climbed many times in winter. It gives a fair, corniced Grade 1 climb.

THE SLUG   180 feet   DIFFICULT

First ascent: Uncertain

This is the forlorn little buttress lying high up under the 3750-foot top of Beinn Mheadoin. It gives an amusing climb on rough but holdless, rounded rock after a good and steep start.

THE LOCH AVON HORSESHOE

Loch Avon lies at a height of 2,377 feet in the heart of the Cairngorms. Not only in this territory renowned for its galaxy of alpine tarns, but in the whole of this country it is unmatched for sheer wildness and grandeur of setting. For nearly two miles it lies entrenched between the crags of Cairngorm and Beinn Mheadhoin. At its head a magnificent cirque of cliffs, shared by Ben Macdhui and Cairngorm, clusters round its main feeder stream, the Garbh Uisge. Dominating this stage are the spectacular, square-topped Shelter Stone Crag (The Sticil) and its perfect foil, sharp-pointed Cairn Etchachan. These are the tallest continuous cliffs (800 feet) in the Cairngorms proper and are justly claimed by Ben Macdhui, the highest Cairngorm summit.

The horseshoe extends from the Cairn Etchachan–Beinn Mheadhoin col to the depression called Coire Raibert on Cairngorm. At two points only is the cliff continuity severed; where the streams Garbh Uisge and Féith Buidhe cascade from the plateau over a slabby, glaciated valley to unite above the loch, and by Coire Domhain, a shallow, grassy depression similar to Coire Raibert.

Cairn Etchachan, the Shelter Stone Crag, and a low line of cliff extending to the Garbh Uisge together form the left leg of the horseshoe. The toe is slab-faced Hell's Lum Crag, 450 feet in height, lying high between the Garbh Uisge and Coire Domhain. The right leg extending along the north shore of the loch is the Stag Rocks, highest at their eastern end where they rise to 600 feet in fine flights of rough granite.

Leading up to this grand cirque on the south side of

Loch Avon is an array of ribs on Beinn Mheadhoin known collectively as the Stacan Dubha. On the north on Cairngorm, from a point near the Saddle, a line of glaciated slabs, the Stac an Fhàraidh, extends to the vicinity of Coire Raibert.

In the distant past large parts of the face of the Shelter Stone Crag have sloughed off leaving gaunt and dizzy sweeps of holdless granite. One of the many huge boulders from these debacles is the Shelter Stone or Clach Dhian, for long the Mecca of many mountaineers. Despite its litter resulting from years of continuous use, it is the best base for climbs in the area. The comfortable capacity is five or six.

In winter, it must always be doubtful if entry could be gained at certain times, therefore the Hutchison Hut should now supersede it as a base in that season. However, under stress, or in case of emergency, it may prove a life-saver.

APPROACHES (to the Shelter Stone)

1. *From Derry Lodge.* By Glen Derry, Coire Etchachan and the Beinn Mheadhoin–Cairn Etchachan col: $6\frac{1}{2}$ miles. 2 miles or 45 minutes from the Hutchison Hut.
2. *From Glenmore Lodge.* The best way unladen is by the Fiacaill Ridge between Coire an Lochain and Coire an t-Sneachda descending by Coire Domhain (unnamed on 1″ map). Follow the stream having its headwater near the summit of Cairn Lochain. Laden, follow the track to the summit of Cairngorm and break off to descend by Coire Raibert: 6 miles.
3. *From Ryvoan Bothy.* Road to Glenmore Lodge, then by 2, or by Strath Nethy and the Saddle.

CAIRN ETCHACHAN

This great, pointed crag, 800 feet in height, is the last of the great faces to have been investigated. Although overshadowed by the unique character of its spectacular neighbour, it yields more climbing. It has two faces: the main face above the loch composed of good rock, and a wall of inferior granite which it hides in Castlegates Gully. The former reputation for loose rock which has been carried by the crag must have been based on observations taken from this gully where in places the wall is indeed loose. The main face, however, is of sound rock.

The main face is interrupted above mid-height by the Great Terrace which can be embarked on and followed without difficulty from the Beinn Mheadhoin col until it vanishes near the junction of the faces. Above and below this terrace, the cliff has differing aspects; the upper cliff where most routes have been made is riven by a bewildering array of vertical ribs, chimneys and cracks, 300 feet in height—the finest feature of the crag; the lower cliff is made up of slabs and slanting ribs bisected by the steep Diagonal Shelf which starts below the Sentinel, a prominent rock mass at the foot of Castlegates Gully, and slants left to meet the Great Terrace.

The Scorpion, one of the longest climbs summer or winter in the Cairngorms, goes up the whole length of the crag from near the Sentinel and passes the end of the Great Terrace to finish in a huge fault which for the sake of convenience is described as the terminating feature of the main face.

The Upper Cliff (Main Face)

A complicated face. Pass along the Great Terrace from the Beinn Mheadhoin col. The first steep buttress houses

Crevasse Route. Then follows a wide, precipitous chimney or gully, Equinox, with a great, overhanging, square tower skylined on its right. On the opposite wall of this tower starting from a shallow, upper amphitheatre is the final, 100-foot crack of Boa. In the opposite corner of this amphitheatre, deeply entrenched in the side of the Python spur, is the upper chimney of the Guillotine. The Python spur is recognised easily by its characteristic pink rock; Boa and the Guillotine routes have a common start on its immediate left. On the right side of the Python spur and hard into the corner formed by it and the face is Nom-de-Plume, a crack-cum-chimney climb. On the face to the right of the Python is Pagan Slit, a long, slanting chimney more prominent from a distance than at close quarters. To the right of the Slit is more pink rock; it should not be confused with the Python spur which is a steeper and more defined feature. The Great Terrace now merges into the face, but ledges trend upwards to the V-shaped recess of the Battlements. By continuing the rightward traverse it is easy to cross from the end of the Terrace to the intermediate section of scrambling on Scorpion.

A little difficulty may be experienced in locating the actual start of the climbs on this Upper Cliff, because (with the exception of Crevasse Route) they commence with several short pitches of a scrambling nature.

CREVASSE ROUTE   250 feet   MILD SEVERE

First ascent: T. W. Patey, M. Smith and A. Duguid
July 29th 1955

The first buttress from the left on the Great Terrace. It has a prominent window high up, well seen from the Beinn Mheadhoin col.

A charming, exhilarating route, giving in its small

compass a varied series of pitches comprising slabs, cracks, chimneys and tunnels.

Start at the lowest rocks; climb steep rock just on the right of mid-line for 60 feet to reach a rock crevasse passing leftwards. 60 feet higher, move into a corner on the right and climb a large, leaning block. The over-hanging, curving crack above is overcome by a layback (crux). To avoid an ensuing, mossy pull-up, step left and climb huge flakes "à cheval" to another crevasse. A queer, contorted chimney of 70 feet exits through a hole to a fine eyrie. Climb the first crack above straight up for 80 feet, veering right at the top up a nose to the true finish of the buttress: an excellent pitch.

EQUINOX 250 feet VERY SEVERE

First ascent: T. W. Patey and L. S. Lovat
October 2nd 1954

To the immediate right of Crevasse Route. Rocks are often greasy.

Indefinite climbing for 100 feet to a huge block at foot of gully proper. Climb the groove for a few feet and step right to continue up shelving slabs on the right of the groove. At 60 feet when this line becomes too steep, make a traverse back to the gully to a block belay. Climb a vertical corner on the right and continue directly up very steep rock for 70 feet (V.S.) to an obvious chimney with a constricted top. Climb the chimney to a platform. Final 20-foot chimney on the left.

BOA 200 feet SEVERE

First ascent: T. W. Patey, F. R. Malcolm and A. Thom
September 25th 1954

Both this route and the Guillotine share a common

start. The rock is excellent and the final crack is magnificently situated.

Zig-zag easily to the foot of the wide chimney of the Guillotine on the immediate left of the Python spur then slant left by ledges and corners towards easier ground in the upper shallow amphitheatre. Move left to foot of 100-foot crack on left wall. This is vertical throughout with a hanging chokestone 70 feet up. Climb by jamming. The movement outwards to pass the block is very exposed.

THE GUILLOTINE   250 feet   VERY DIFFICULT

First ascent: T. W. Patey and A. Duguid *August 13th 1955*

Start as for Boa, but enter the wide chimney (often wet). Climb it direct and continue into the upper amphitheatre.

It is now easy to join Python above the great, semi-detached flake on that route. However, instead of taking the first chimney on the right (as on Python), move up to the next. This chimney, which cuts sharply into the spur on the right, is initially very deep behind a large flake, and then climbs steeply up as a fine tunnel roofed by jammed blocks. At the top there is a good platform below the final 60-foot chimney of Python route (M.S.).

PYTHON   250 feet   VERY SEVERE

First ascent: T. W. Patey and L. S. Lovat

October 2nd 1954

On the spur of pink rock in the centre of the Upper Cliff. A strenuous route with sustained difficulty.

Pass along below the spur and make a start on the far,

west side aiming for a huge semi-detached flake set high on the face. A few feet up, a 20-foot slanting cleft cuts a wall of red rock. There is a large platform on its right at the start. Jam up the cleft (S.) to a mossy platform and jumble of rocks. The next pitch on the right leads in 50 feet to a crack behind the great flake. It starts as a strenuous layback (V.S.) and continues with a stiff pull over an overhang (V.S.). "A cheval" to the top of the flake.

Walk left below a smooth wall to east side of spur opposite Boa. Climb the first chimney on the right to a large platform on the spur (80 feet). The final wall is above a great fang of rock. Climb the central chimney, 60 feet (M.S.).

NOM-DE-PLUME   250 feet   VERY SEVERE (V.)

First ascent: R. W. P. Barclay and R. H. Sellers

August 12th 1956

The chimney-crack in the angle formed by the right side of the Python spur and the face.

Jam up a vertical chimney filled with small chokestones then climb on to right wall with final layback to platform and belay below a narrow 6-foot chimney split into two cracks with a fang of rock above (60 feet, S.). Climb the short chimney (strenuous) then pull over on to fang comprising floor of overhang. Move right using holds on overhang (thread) on to grass platform (V.S.). Continue by mantelshelf ledges to large platform (100 feet). Climb, following deep-cut constricting chimney, to huge diamond-shaped block. Pass block on left wall to a platform and final pitch of Python.

PAGAN SLIT   250 feet   HARD SEVERE

First ascent: G. Adams and R. W. P. Barclay
August 7th 1955

Between the spur of Python and some more pink rock next to the Battlements.

A prominent, slanting chimney inclining rightwards and broken by several mossy, overhanging ledges. It has several hard pitches and is best suited for dry weather.

A narrow 20-foot chimney to a large, grassy terrace. Continue up the chimney with difficulty sustained by a series of chokestones for 50 feet. For the next 80 feet the chimney is easier and widens in parts with two avoidable through-routes leading on to a grassy scoop below the final wall. Continue up the main chimney with a step on to a precarious flake. After 80 feet move right to a stance behind a flake boulder. Step back into the chimney and climb strenuously for a few feet. Easier climbing to the top.

THE BATTLEMENTS   300 feet   MODERATE

First ascent: T. W. Patey and W. D. Brooker
August 10th 1954

Once accurately located this route provides a handy means of descent to gain access to the climbs on the Upper Cliff.

Near the end of the Great Terrace the Upper Cliff becomes more broken. From near the end of the terrace ledges trend naturally upwards to a large V groove with a ladder of holds on its right wall. At the top of the groove easier climbing leftwards for 200 feet leads directly to the top of Cairn Etchachan.

The Lower Cliff (Main Face)

The face below the Great Terrace. It is cut by the steep Diagonal Shelf which commences just below the jammed-blocks gully to the left of Scorpion. A direct line from the lowest point of the face to the summit of Cairn Etchachan is followed by Route Major, the longest recorded winter climb in the Cairngorms. The only other climb using the face is the Eastern Approach Route to the Great Terrace.

EASTERN APPROACH ROUTE 350 feet DIFFICULT

First ascent: T. W. Patey   *July 29th 1955*

Start just to the right of a belt of slabs at the bottom left-hand corner of the crag. Cross left by a trap-dyke above the slabs, then continue up and slightly rightwards by a variety of minor pitches, some of them awkward and vegetated, to reach the Terrace in the vicinity of Crevasse Route.

ROUTE MAJOR   850 feet to cairn   GRADE 4

First ascent: T. W. Patey and M. Smith *February 10th 1957*

The longest and one of the finest winter climbs on record in the Cairngorms, following a central line from the lowest rocks and finishing at the summit cairn. In its upper part it borrows the Battlements groove. The lower part is not a summer climb. Sustained high-angle; route-finding; fine situations—a mountaineering route.

Starting from the snow basin to the right of the lowest rocks the party of the first ascent followed an ascending band of snow slanting left for about 200 feet, then traversed back sharp right along a shelf ending in a steep corner. Ascent of the corner led to a snow bay with a

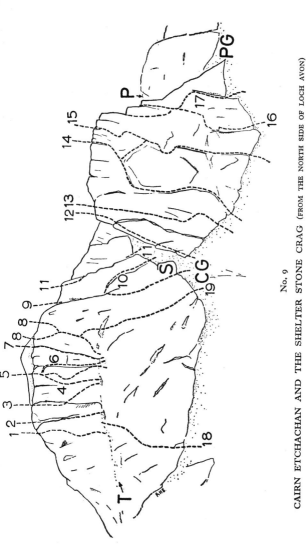

No. 9

CAIRN ETCHACHAN AND THE SHELTER STONE CRAG (FROM THE NORTH SIDE OF LOCH AVON)

T—Terrace   CG—Castlegates Gully   S—Sentinel   PG—Pinnacle Gully   P—Forefinger Pinnacle

1—Crevasse Route
2—Equinox
3—Boa...

6—Nom-de-Plume
7—Pagan Slit
8—The Battlements

11—Castle Gully
12—Castle Wall
13—Raeburn's Buttress

16—Postern
17—Clach Dhian Chimney
18—Eastern Approach Route

deep, tapering chimney on its left margin. The chimney was climbed and its constricted top avoided by an awkward exit on to the iced slab on the left. An easier groove led to steep, mixed terrain below the upper cliff. Here the line of least resistance goes up rightwards towards the summer crux-groove of the Battlements (unseen from below). The party made a long traverse across crests and troughs of snow to the right followed by an upward move leading to a rib. The rib was climbed, then crossed and a short descent made into the main trough leading to the Battlements Groove (four run-outs from the top of the constricted chimney). The groove gave a very steep 50-foot ice-pitch (crux). A break-out left and a steep upward traverse leftwards for 120 feet led to a short rock-wall climbed by an iced crack in its lower margin. A fine finish up steep convex slopes to the cairn. Time on first ascent with iron-hard snow 3½ hours. The axe required for every step. It would be well to allow 6–8 hours for a two-party with the route under deep powder.

The Gully Face

THE BOUNDARY LINE separating the main face from the gully face is followed by Scorpion, a route starting below the Sentinel, a rock mass at the foot of Castlegates Gully. This gully face is not cut by terraces but the climbing is inferior to that on the main face; there are stretches of good rock but much loose debris lies on ledges.

On the immediate right of Scorpion commencing above the Sentinel an indefinite gully called False Scorpion cuts into the cliff and ends to the right of the upper fault of Scorpion. Next up Castlegates Gully one passes a great ridge to reach the only other recorded route on this face—Castle Gully, a slabby, indefinite recess opening out beyond a curious, red cave on the left wall.

The great ridge so well seen in profile from the Shelter Stone, although not climbed throughout, is used in its upper narrow portion by Castle Gully route.

SCORPION   700 feet   VERY DIFFICULT. GRADE 5

First ascent (winter): T. W. Patey, J. M. Taylor, A. G. Nicol
     and K. A. Grassick   *December 6th 1952*
First summer ascent: H. S. M. Bates and T. Shaw
                                          May 10th 1953

First ascent made under snow and ice, providing a magnificent climb of 7 hours duration. When snow-free the line of the winter route affords one of the longest rock climbs in the Cairngorms. Little artificiality, but the selection of the best line is difficult. Sustained interest over a variety of pitches.

Start up a steep, mossy corner to the left of a V groove about 50 feet below the Sentinel, midway between it and a gully housing some huge blocks. At 60 feet continue left for 30 feet beneath a steep wall. The wall is cut by a slanting crack. Enter the crack after 10 feet; the route is now subterranean. Above the exit, climb an overhung wall on the immediate right on good holds (M.S.), and shortly above pass round a corner to the right and go up on a leftward line to cross left over a slab by a crack in its lower margin.

Route is now evident for 150 feet to easy ground below the upper fault. This is steep and twists, forming a gully in its last 200 feet. (At its foot a steep cracked shelf leads up on to Battlements route on the left.)

The fault starts as a long chimney designed for straddling; slabs above the chimney lead into its gully section. Climb the arête on the right for 80 feet to avoid a big pitch (the winter crux), and continue up the groove in the corner for 6o feet to exit across the right wall by an easy ledge to a small tower and easy ground.

Winter: Mainly powder-snow encountered on the first ascent. Crux was the big ice-pitch in the upper fault. In the absence of a snow take-off this was extremely hard. 65° snow above this to the exit. Ideal conditions might occur in early spring with a combination of bare rock on the lower section and an adequate deposit of snow in the upper fault. Allow at least 5 hours for a two-party. (E.C.J. 2.145.)

FALSE SCORPION   700 feet   VERY DIFFICULT

First ascent: K. A. Grassick, H. S. M. Bates, A. Q. Gardiner and A. Farquharson   *August 1952*

A much inferior route to Scorpion. Rock very loose in the lower gully.

It starts above the Sentinel and follows a depression or shallow gully which narrows and steepens to a crack. At this point it diverges left by an upward traverse over vegetated slabs and crosses over a rib into the upper fault of Scorpion at a point where the fault bends. It then follows that route to the plateau.

The unclimbed continuation of the gully opens out and veers right to end at the plateau to the right of, and separated from Scorpion by a series of steep ribs.

CASTLE GULLY   450 feet   VERY DIFFICULT

First ascent: H. S. M. Bates, K. A. Grassick and A. G. Nicol   *May 24th 1952*

Go up Castlegates Gully for 250 feet from the Sentinel, passing the great ridge on the left. Castle Gully then opens out beyond a red cave on the left wall. The lower

H

section is open and slabby; higher up it narrows to a steep 30-foot chimney. Above this, climb an overhung layback crack of 12 feet on the left (M.S.) leading to the rib of the great ridge about 200 feet from the top. Follow the crest—steep and interesting.

CASTLEGATES GULLY   600 feet   EASY.   GRADE I

First ascent: H. Stewart and A. B. Duncan   *July 1904*
First winter ascent: J. McCoss, W. B. Meff, R. Clarke and
    W. Shepherd   *Easter 1914*

This well-known thoroughfare separates the Shelter Stone Crag from Cairn Etchachan. It harbours one short, easy pitch. There is good rock-scenery. Care required on the descent by a large party because of large, unstable scree. Rock-hard snow usually found low in the gully far into summer. (J. 8.183.)

Winter: Straightforward 40° snow steepening at the exit. Cornice may be heavy, but is not usually so. (C.C.J. 14.365.)

SHELTER STONE CRAG

This 800-foot table-topped cliff (sometime known as the Sticil) is the most fascinating and most unaccommodating in the Cairngorms, also without doubt one of the finest, steepest and most imposing crags on British mountains. There are few chinks in its grim armour. The Central Slabs which form its heart, nearly 500 feet of unjointed granite, are manifestly impossible. This is also the case with much of the rock forming the great vertical bastion to the right of Central Slabs, unless mechanised techniques are employed to excess. Only on the fringes of these features does the granite relent.

The crag thrusts out boldly between Castlegates Gully on the left and Pinnacle Gully on the right. It has two faces; the great north face merging into the small, triangular west face overlooking Pinnacle Gully. The rock at the eastern end of the north face between Central Slabs and Castlegates Gully is vegetated; on the bastion to the right of Central Slabs it is too clean—massive in formation, with few lines of weakness and lacking in holds. The west face is more weathered, consequently holds are more plentiful, but in places they require careful handling.

Six routes have been made: (1) Castle Wall, the easy-angled rib alongside Castlegates Gully; (2) Raeburn's Buttress, the well-defined, steep pillar between Castle Wall and the Central Slabs; (3) Sticil Face, a climb following the line of weakness running up the right side of Raeburn's Buttress and crossing above the Central Slabs to finish in a chimney cutting into the left side of the great bastion near the plateau; (4) The Citadel which follows the conspicuous chimney on the right of Central Slabs then diverges right above its overhangs on to the vertical promontory jutting out from the great bastion; (5) Postern, starting near the lowest rocks and after the lower slabs are passed going up to the upper of two steps on the right skyline by chimney-faults to finish thereafter on the hidden face overlooking Pinnacle Gully; (6) Clach Dhian Chimney, starting in a gully on the right of the crag and finishing on the Pinnacle Gully face after reaching the lower skyline step.

There may yet be other lines of attack on the vertical bastion between the Citadel and Postern but all is very problematical and intimidating. Undoubtedly a great challenge is a direct finish by the stupendous 100-foot hanging crack cleaving the perpendicular rocks midway between the Citadel and the right skyline. From surveys on very hard sorties from Postern it appears that it will just admit a climber and a chink of light seen from directly below seems to indicate a through-route near the plateau.

CASTLE WALL 600 feet DIFFICULT

First ascent: H. Raeburn and F. S. Goggs *June 16th 1907*

Starting at the foot of Castlegates Gully a well-defined arête is climbed for 200 feet. There is more than one awkward pitch and the rock should be handled carefully. A cairn is reached on the arête where parties have sidled in from the gully. Above this the climbing becomes indefinite, and scrambling follows for a long way to the top of the crag.

RAEBURN'S BUTTRESS 650 feet SEVERE

First ascent: H. Raeburn and F. S. Goggs *June 16th 1907*

The pioneer party were of the opinion that the climb was dangerous—it is still so. All the 500 feet up to the square-cut shoulder is on extremely steep rock veiled with vegetation. The crux is especially dangerous. Leave it severely alone in wet weather.

The climbing is on the Castle Wall side of the buttress. Follow an obvious line of vegetated cracks for about 150 feet, then traverse the buttress in the direction of Castle Wall arête. From this ledge follow another and more defined line of weakness to the shoulder for 350 feet. Above the short, level shoulder no further difficulty of note is encountered. (J. 10.10.)

The crux occurs at a point where the right-hand line is abandoned. The first move on the traverse necessitates a long stride on to a disintegrating shelflet of grass (S.). There is no secure belay. Use a piton for safeguard.

STICIL FACE   700 feet   HARD SEVERE.   GRADE 5

First ascent: J. M. Taylor and T. W. Patey *May 14th 1953*
First winter ascent: K. A. Grassick and A. G. Nicol
December 27th 1957

A route following the angle between the Central Slabs
and Raeburn's Buttress alongside an indefinite, slabby
gully. The promenade across and up the High Ledge
provides a satisfying downward view over the dizzy
Central Slabs. Much vegetation. Avoid when wet.

Gain a series of grass ledges from a point below and to
the right of Raeburn's Buttress. These slant across the
face above the lower belt of slabs forming the Low Ledge
leading into the chimney of the Citadel. Leave the
ledges behind and go up left for 160 feet by awkward,
grassy steps to a platform with a large, flake belay. The
platform is just to the left of the slabby gully which is
wet and holdless at this point. Climb from the flake the
40-foot steep edge directly above (crux) to a ledge, then
a 30-foot V groove. Hence by easy ledges return right
to the gully which continues as a steep chimney. Easy
above. The shoulder of Raeburn's Buttress can now be
reached but the route diverges to the right across the
face above the Central Slabs by the long slanting High
Ledge to gain an intriguing 100-foot, deep-cut chimney
cleaving the left side of the promontory of the great
bastion.

Winter: An excellent climb of sustained severity. The
slabby gully of summer is a natural ice-trap and will
always be extremely hard. The character of the climb
is enhanced by the passage of the High Ledge which, due
to the snow-banking, becomes a lengthy exposed traverse. On the first ascent there were three ice-pitches
in the gully. The first was turned on the left by snow-
covered rocks. The second, a 70-foot ice-fall, was also

passed on the left by a 100-foot run-out up a V groove. The third (crux) was an ice-choked chimney climbed direct using two pitons. The final 100-foot chimney of summer was not climbed; instead, the party traversed right from its foot underneath an overhang and then used combined tactics on the ensuing 12-foot wall. Above this an arête of snow led to the plateau. Time: 9 hours.

THE CITADEL   800 feet   VERY SEVERE (V.)

First ascent: R. H. Sellers and G. Annand   *August 1958*

The most direct route on the crag to date. On its upper section it is in a most splendid environment, providing exposed climbing of great character, but technique in artificial climbing is required. The lower section follows the conspicuous chimney bounding the right side of Central Slabs; the upper is on the steep nose dominating the left side of the great bastion. This nose is in line with the apparent highest point and is characterised by a huge, overhanging, blank wall cut by a slanting crack.

Start initially up grassy cracks giving two long pitches leading to the Low Ledge. Here the chimney proper is entered. Climb three straightforward pitches (V.D.) passing the Gallery on the right up to greasy overhangs which force an exit on to a ledge on left (piton belay). The crux of the lower section follows. From the ledge go a little left then over small ledges and make a 10-foot right traverse to a "dièdre" with a crack on right wall just next the overhangs. Climb the "dièdre" by layback to an overhang. Move up on this using a piton then swing right on another piton 8 feet higher on to a small hold on lip of overhang; thence climb a slab and go

right to the foot of a grass fault with belay stance on left
(120 feet). Climb a wall on right then the grass fault to
a large stance and piton belay. Grassy ledges and
terraces now lead up easily to the High Ledge of Sticil
Face but the route goes right on to the great nose.

From the top of the grass fault traverse right into an
obvious corner. Continue up the corner and the chimney
into which it develops to gain a ridge with stance and
piton belay (100 feet, M.S.). Follow ridge for 60 feet
then traverse left over a nose and up to a stance alongside a large flake butting the huge, overhanging wall in
front (70 feet, V.D.). The hardest pitch follows. There
is no way ahead so make a sensational hand traverse for
15 feet to the left and mantelshelf on to a block (piton
runner), thence go up an awkward crack (wooden
wedge) to another and overhanging crack on a smooth
wall. Use stirrups for the crack and at the top make a
very delicate move into a chimney followed to a good
stance and piton belay (60 feet, V.S.). Now traverse up
right following the rim of the overhanging wall then up
to a ledge with loose block (60 feet, M.S.). Steep but
easy climbing in the ensuing fault follows until two
10-foot chimneys are reached. Climb that on the left to
summit (V.D.).

POSTERN   750 feet   HARD SEVERE (V.)

First ascent Lower Section: J. Y. L. Hay and G. Adams
                                        September 1956
First ascent Upper Section: K. A. Grassick, A. G. Nicol and
    J. G. Lillie   *June 16th 1957*

The outcome of an attempt on a direct ascent from
the lowest rocks. Rather exposed and bewildering in
its upper section. Starts near the lowest rocks and

finishes on the hidden west face after gaining the upper step on the right skyline. Through a combination of foreshortening and recession these steps appear to be set lower on the cliff than is actually the case—a curious effect.

The salient features are (*A*) the Gallery, a narrow terrace (not seen from directly below) leading right from the chimney of the Citadel across the top of the lower slabs to the start (250 feet) of (*B*) the Slanting Crack, an obvious intermittent fault going up to the lower step on the right skyline.

To the right of the lowest point of the crag a series of "dièdres" one above the other but not in line, breaks the continuity of the slabs. Start in an open grassy chimney to the right of the lowest "dièdre". Go up 80 feet till stopped by a vertical wall. Traverse left 15 feet to a piton belay. Continue up a corner then go left to a ledge at the base of a long right-angled "dièdre". Progress upwards for 35 feet is hard; there are fine cracks on the upright but the floor is devoid of holds (H.S., two pitons for direct aid). At the top break out right to a belay. Above this easier climbing leads to the Gallery. Traverse right to the Slanting Crack (less obvious from here than from below). The first pitch is slightly overhanging but the holds are good (M.S.). Climb the Crack, here virtually a shelf, for a further 150 feet by slab and wall pitches (D.) to where Clach Dhian Chimney route comes in from the right "en route" for the lower step on the Skyline. Here there is a deep 30-foot chimney cleaving the left wall. Climb the chimney and traverse left to a long wall and groove pitch which ends at a narrow ledge (H.S.). A short left catwalk followed by an obvious trend right lands one at the upper step on the right skyline. The step is the apex of a slabby staircase ascending from the Pinnacle Gully face. Inset in a corner at the apex and bounded on its left by a sheer wall with a prominent jutting block is a fine, unclimbed chimney. Go past the chimney and climb to the plateau by a steep, slabby shelf on its right side (90 feet, V.D., the last pitch of Clach Dhian Chimney).

CLACH DHIAN CHIMNEY 650 feet VERY DIFFICULT

First ascent: W. S. Thomson and party *August 27th 1947*

This is the West Wall Route of C.G.1950 (p. 183). The account therein of the pioneers is lacking in detail. They evidently failed to follow the chimney throughout, and their route on the upper section is open to conjecture. The route now used is that followed and named by W. D. Brooker and J. W. Morgan (1950). In its upper section it enters the Slanting Crack used by Postern and follows it out to the lower step on the skyline. Its final pitch is also used by Postern. Care required on some sections, nevertheless a fine route for a competent party. Splendid situations.

Start in the obvious, wide chimney to the left of the foot of Pinnacle Gully. Climb the first chokestone pitch by a crack on the left (V.D.) leading into a groove followed by easy ground. (Pioneers evaded this pitch on the right (M.).) Go up two more very difficult pitches to a point where the chimney, here virtually a gully, ends below a steep wall. Make an exit to the left (V.D.) and for the next 200 feet zig-zag upwards towards the vertical upper wall of the crag to meet an easy, but sensational, horizontal shelf leading into the Slanting Crack of Postern. Follow out the Crack to the lower step on the skyline. Now tackle the final wall overlooking Pinnacle Gully by the obvious fan-shaped slab-staircase leading to the final pitch which is also that of Postern (q.v.).

PINNACLE GULLY   600 feet   EASY.   GRADE I

First ascent: H. Stewart and A. B. Duncan   *July 1904*

A wide, scree corridor, remarkable only for having the Forefinger Pinnacle at its head. At the top there are wet slabs, easy in the right corner (J. 8.183).

Winter: A simple snow climb amidst good scenery. No record of first party.

FOREFINGER PINNACLE

First ascent: H. G. Drummond and J. McCoss   *July 1912*

Aptly named by the first visitors to the gully. This curious rock-formation—unique for Cairngorm granite—looks impressive when seen from below. It bears a striking resemblance to a hand with the index finger pointing heavenward, breaking the skyline at the head of Pinnacle Gully (photograph C.G. 1950, p. 174).

It has been climbed on all sides, the routes varying from 30 feet on its upper side to 100 feet on its lower. The routes are:

(a) The normal route up the back, or short side, by an obvious crack between the main wall and the subsidiary buttress on the right. Moderate.

(b) 10 feet to the left of normal route. Climb face directly, close to corner. Difficult.

(c) By the face opposing the Shelter Stone Crag. Difficult.

(d) The west face. Dangerous hanging blocks at mid-height. Hard severe.

(e) From the lowest point in the gully, stepping left when the face becomes very steep to finish by a crack on east face. Very difficult.

(*f*) Direct ascent from lowest point. The finest route. Moderate rock to large block. Move up left edge of vertical wall then traverse right to shelf. 20 feet hard climbing to right of prominent crack to triangular shelf then final pitch up shallow chimney overhanging at bottom (combined tactics). 110 feet. Severe.

THE GRADUAL transition from the vertical of the Shelter Stone Crag to the tamer angles of the glaciated hollow holding the Avon headwaters is effected by a palisade of cliff upwards of 200 feet in height rising steeply to the right of Pinnacle Gully in small buttresses cleft by gullies.

The rock is rather broken to give continuous climbing but one route is recorded. A defined little rib rises on the extreme right separated from the main mass by a slab-filled gully containing a big quartz vein. It gives 200 feet of fair climbing. (T. W. Patey on the descent, August 1954).

HELL'S LUM CRAG

The steep, smooth cliff lying high to the right of the Féith Buidhe and facing out along Loch Avon. Perfect rock, unaccountably neglected in the past.

The crag's name is derived from a huge rift in its left side which cannot be seen from the Shelter Stone and should not be confused with Deep-Cut Chimney which is conspicuous from that viewpoint cleaving the frontal slabs as a thin, black line with a curious right-angled twist at its foot.

The slabs to the left of the Lum are usually wet and have no climbs. Between the Lum and Deep-Cut Chimney is an imposing, unclimbed buttress which is in the process of becoming a huge, detached tower—a curious chimney, the Pothole, cuts through the crag from the Lum to meet Deep-Cut Chimney on the opposite side. The two climbs are thinly separated, but the cleavage at the plateau is perfect although roofed in by boulders.

On the frontal face Deep-Cut Chimney is almost duplicated by another fault. To the right of this fault in a recess is Hellfire Corner. In a central position going up above the lowest rocks is Devil's Delight, a face climb, and on the right section of the crag is Kiwi Slabs, a route following a shallow gully in the centre section. Finally beyond Kiwi Slabs is the Escalator, an obvious watercourse.

HELL'S LUM   350 feet   GRADE 2–3

First ascent: I. M. Brooker and Miss M. Newbigging
April 19th 1952
First winter ascent: G. McLeod and A. N. Other
March 1956

There has been no true summer ascent of this gully; all attempts being stopped nearly half-way up by one of the most impressive gully pitches in the Cairngorms—a 60-foot vertical face over which water pours. There is no way of turning the obstacle and the faults in either corner look fierce.

In summer a number of big overhanging blocks fill the lower gully. These are turned by a steep slab-shelf on the right, climbed close to the right wall and awkward at the top. Above, scree leads to the unclimbed pitch. On the first ascent (in near summer conditions) steep snow covered the lower pitches and provided a take-off for the great pitch which was masked for half its height: 30 feet of very difficult, wet but sound rock. Above

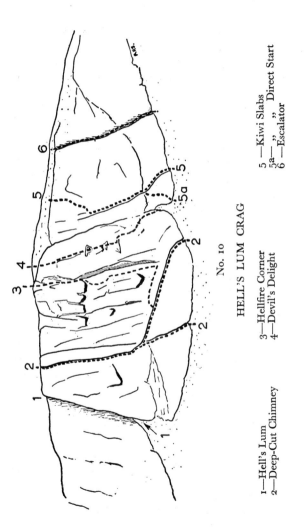

No. 10

HELL'S LUM CRAG

1 —Hell's Lum
2 —Deep-Cut Chimney

3 —Hellfire Corner
4 —Devil's Delight

5 —Kiwi Slabs
5a — ,,   ,,   Direct Start
6 —Escalator

came slabs interspersed with snow leading to another difficult rock-pitch of 40 feet. Following this, very steep snow and ice led to the last pitch, 30 feet of poor rock on the right.

Winter: Though variable, a recommended climb in a splendid environment—grand snow scenery. In mid-season it may carry three pitches averaging 25 feet in height. At peak in a good year usually no pitches are visible, but it is high-angled, always heavily corniced and there is often the menace of falls from an ice-curtain which clings to the left wall.

THE POTHOLE   150 feet   VERY DIFFICULT

First ascent and descent: R. W. P. Barclay and R. H. Sellers
October 21st 1956

Situated above the great pitch in Hell's Lum and going through the right wall to meet Deep-Cut Chimney on the other side. A curious formation. Vertical.

Go right into the back of the chimney sometimes as much as 25 feet and climb by back and knee or jamming. All the chokestones are safe.

DEEP-CUT CHIMNEY   400 feet   VERY DIFFICULT
GRADE 4

First ascent: I. M. Brooker and Miss M. Newbigging
September 1950
First winter ascent: T. W. Patey and D. Holroyd
January 19th 1958

An impressive slit, vegetated in its lower part, but with walls close enough for using back and feet to avoid the greenery. A good climb with a spectacular and un-expected finish.

Start either directly below or by the easy terraced

fault cleaving the smooth, lower slabs. Once in the chimney proper there are a number of pitches to be overcome, mostly fern and grass-grown—hence climb them back and foot leaving the herbage untouched. About 150 feet from the top the rock scenery becomes quite remarkable; the chimney cuts far into the cliff and chokestones are jammed well out between the walls forming a tunnel. Back and foot outwards below the final overhang to reach a crazy pile of boulders wedged in the outer jaws. The finish comes with startling suddenness.

Winter: A fine ice-route bearing some resemblance to Comb Gully of Nevis but much more sustained. On the first ascent in unfavourable conditions two feet of recent powder overlay ice. Introductory slabs were covered. The lower chimney contained three ice-pitches (all V.S.). The upper part of the climb was relatively straightforward as excellent hard-packed snow lined the back of the chimney. Time: 3 hours.

HELLFIRE CORNER   400 feet   SEVERE (V.)

First ascent: G. Annand and R. H. Sellers
September 14th 1958

A recessed section of the cliff to the right of Deep-Cut and beyond its duplicating fault forms a great corner running up on a slight diagonal to the right. This is the route. A first-rate climb on clean, waterwashed rock, but often wet.

Start up the terraced fault as for Deep-Cut. At the top cut back right across a glacis, descending slightly till a slab is reached which has a crack leading to the corner. Go up the crack for 20 feet then follow corner till a block forces a climb on the right wall then return. A further 20 feet up there is a stance and belay (120 feet). A series of steps in the corner are now climbed followed by an excursion on to the left wall for 10 feet to reach a crack. Climb crack for 15 feet then mantelshelf and traverse right to poor stance and piton belay (60 feet). Continue right to attain corner again then up a sharp arête to beneath breach in the overhangs. Chimney through this with chokestones for aid at the lip of bulge then move up right to slab (50 feet). Ascend a big cave pitch on left and follow easy chimneys and a grassy fault to summit (180 feet).

DEVIL'S DELIGHT   450 feet   HARD SEVERE (v.)

First ascent: R. H. Sellers and G. Annand *August 4th 1957*

Between Hellfire Corner and a discontinuous gully just right of the lowest rocks is a fine section of cliff marked by the Haven, a prominent green ledge about half-way up. The route follows a line of thin cracks almost on a centre line and crosses the Haven. The best route on the crag but, as with Hellfire Corner, often wet, even in dry weather.

The lower slabs are glaciated and holdless and the start is in the discontinuous gully. Climb gully for 50 feet then move left along small ledge on the slabs then up a crack and rib to a corner (piton belay). Climb the corner and crack above to finish on rock glacis. Move left to a big recess in glacis. From the top of a 10-foot block climb the vertical wall in front by laybacking and jamming up a crack with a delicate mantelshelf exit (piton belay, 80 feet, M.S.). Climb two short walls to a triangular niche and leave by a strenuous, overhanging wet crack of 15 feet which leads to the Haven. Now follow three fine pitches. Climb up cracks for 20 feet, then by a recess to a stance beneath bulge (piton belay). Scale the wall on left and swing into a crack in the bulge

(H.S.), continuing to a second bulge. Here one can either traverse 5 feet right to another crack or go over the bulge (H.S.) to a chimney recess behind a huge, 30-foot detached block (90 feet). The angle now eases. Finish by going straight up by a crack and then a staircase (90 feet).

KIWI SLABS   350 feet   VERY DIFFICULT. GRADE 4

First ascent: R. Naylor and M. W. Parkin
August 8th 1953
First winter ascent: T. W. Patey and V. N. Stevenson
February 1959

Mid-way between the lowest point of the crag and the Coire Domhain burn there is a prominent, square-cut, green buttress. The original start (which is rather artificial) goes up its left edge; the easier and more logical route follows an obvious rake commencing some distance to the right. Particularly smooth granite. (J. 25.247.)

Follow the rake slanting left to the foot of a gully for 100 feet (M.). (This cuts out the initial three pitches of the original start.) The gully starts with two 80-foot pitches then steepens considerably. Break out on the right wall by a short crack followed by a ledge leading to a chimney. Cave and spike belay 10 feet up. Just above the cave step right round an exposed corner to a ledge (crux). An awkward slab follows, then the final 50-foot wall.

Original Start: Zig-zag up the left edge of the square-cut buttress for 25 feet to a ledge. Now go along a diagonal crack for 25 feet by a fine hand traverse to the tip of the buttress (M.S.). Above is a wet corner formed by a slab with an overhung wall on its left. Climb this to reach the foot of the gully (1 piton in place, H.S.).

I

Winter: Summer route followed on first ascent. Apart from the first two pitches which were obliterated and the hard pitch on the upper section which was bare rock, the ascent was made entirely on thin ice-ribbons. A fine route. Time: 1½ hours.

THE ESCALATOR   300 feet   MODERATE. GRADE 3

First ascent: A. G. Nicol, T. W. Patey and Miss E. M.
    Davidson   *September 30th 1955*
First winter ascent: J. Y. L. Hay and A. Thom
                                         January 1960

The obvious watercourse to the right of Kiwi Slabs. Clean rock but best in dry weather. A good training climb.

Easy scrambling up a gully leads to a large platform below the steeper section where an easy shelf leads off to the right. Three or four rope-lengths of good climbing follow, finishing just to the left of the watercourse.

Winter: No details available.

The Crag in winter. The crag, open to the sun, bears an alpine appearance in winter and spring with berg-schrunds opening up on the lower slabs and ice masking the sector between Deep-Cut Chimney and Kiwi Slabs. This ice, particularly heavy on the steep buttress holding Devil's Delight, seems to be formed by water issuing from hidden springs among the upper rocks. The companion chimney of Deep-Cut would repay a visit, as would the intermittent gully on the left of Kiwi Slabs.

THE STAG ROCKS

The collective name for the cliffs opposite the Shelter Stone Crag, belonging to Cairngorm. They have a

southern exposure and their rock is rough so that climbing here is more light-hearted than elsewhere in the
Horseshoe. There are two main sections of cliff separated
by Diagonal Gully, a long shoot sending its screes almost
to the loch.

THE LEFT SECTION

This is composed of well-defined arêtes, ribs and subsidiary ridges giving pleasant, unpretentious climbs of
which there are four recorded.

AFTERTHOUGHT ARÊTE   450 feet   MODERATE

First ascent: R. H. Sellers and M. Smith   *September 1956*

This is the leftmost and most regularly shaped arête of
the section. It bounds the right side of a wide, scree
gully. The first pitch from the lowest rocks is surprisingly
difficult but can be avoided. After this the rocks develop
into an excellent, steep knife-edge for 250 feet and
maintain their interest to the top.

QUARTZ-DIGGERS' CAVE ROUTE   250 feet
VERY DIFFICULT

First ascent: R. H. Sellers, G. Adams and F. Henderson
June 1957

On the buttress to the immediate right of Afterthought
can be seen the cave. This is an artificial cave hollowed
out by the gemstone seekers of the past.

The climb starts on the rib to the left of the cave and
20 feet beneath the entrance. Follow the rib till forced
on to an open corner climbed on right wall to stance
(100 feet). Climb a wall on small flake holds then
shallow groove with a small overhang to a stance (100

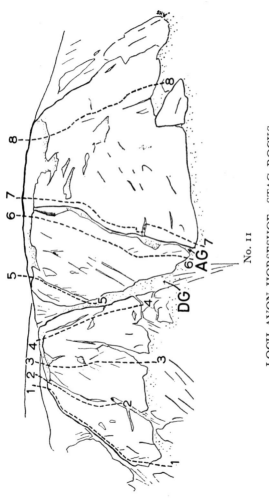

LOCH AVON HORSESHOE: STAG ROCKS

No. 11

DG—Diagonal Gully   AG—Amphitheatre Gully

1—Afterthought Arête   3—Triple Towers   5—Final Selection   7—The Relay Climb
2—Quartz-Diggers' Cave Route 4—Serrated Rib   6—Pine Tree Route   8—The Tenements

feet). From here either go straight up slabs or traverse left into grassy groove and follow crest to top (75 feet). The main rib finishes here but another rib 100 feet long running parallel gives a good scramble.

TRIPLE TOWERS   400 feet   MODERATE

First ascent: T. W. Patey and G. B. Leslie   *August 1954*

The right boundary of the section is Serrated Rib which overlooks Diagonal Gully. Triple Towers lies to the left of Serrated Rib across a deep, constricted gully.

The three towers form a discontinuous rib and each of them is climbed directly up its right edge, or close to it on moderate rock.

SERRATED RIB   400 feet   MODERATE

First ascent: J. B. Nimlin and party   *July 1930*

Forms the left wall of Diagonal Gully. As seen from the Shelter Stone it appears to have a square-cut causeway at the top. Mostly easy scrambling although difficulties can be found by starting at the left corner. Higher up it narrows to an arête on its left edge. Keep to the left edge.

DIAGONAL GULLY (chiefly scree) is steep enough to give a long glissade in winter.

THE RIGHT SECTION

The rocks here are more massive and the section is itself divided into two crags by the big Amphitheatre Gully which is open-walled on the left and houses three big pitches. The subsidiary on the left which harbours two routes is Pine Tree Buttress. The greater one on the right is Longbow Crag, 600 feet high and most defined on its Amphitheatre Gully edge. This edge is followed throughout by the Relay Climb, the best route to date on the Stag Rocks. Further right beyond the broad, slabby front of the crag is the Tenements a route on the detached rib bolstering up the right flank.

Pine Tree Buttress

PINE TREE ROUTE   500 feet   DIFFICULT

First ascent: E. L. Smith and R. Mennie   *July 17th 1949*

A pleasant climb on good rock on a broad and defined rib going up from the lowest rocks and overlooking Amphitheatre Gully.

Start at the foot up a long tongue of broken rock. Above this the route gradually diverges right to the Gully. Just before the edge is reached pass round a corner on the left then carry straight up bearing right up a corner. Near the top a steep, clean wall on the left of the crest enables one to turn a huge overhang. The climb ends at an easy 20-foot wall.

FINAL SELECTION   200 feet   DIFFICULT

First ascent: R. H. Sellers and M. Smith   *November 1956*

From Diagonal Gully many grooves and arêtes slant up the left side of the buttress. This short climb is on the last defined arête not far from the top of the Gully. The right side is vertical, the left side is slab angling steeply into a shallow gully.

Start up a short chimney (the foot of the shallow gully) from an awkward move on the left. Once in the gully break out right on to the arête. Continue on the arête till pushed off on to the cracked slabs on the left. Good, steep climbing on these lead up right over a neck to a platform. An easy chimney leads to the top.

AMPHITHEATRE GULLY because of its open left wall has little interest in summer apart from its final pitch which forms a big defined corner.

Longbow Crag

THE RELAY CLIMB   6oo feet   VERY SEVERE (V.)

First ascents—Upper Section: K. Winram   *August 1953*
Lower Section: G. H. Leslie and M. Smith
June 1954
Middle Section: T. W. Patey   *August 1955*

On the edge of Amphitheatre Gully. An interesting climb on good rock with one very hard pitch on a transverse bulge on the cliff at the start of the middle section. Several attempts at three different points on the bulge had been made before a solution was found. The Longbow from which the crag is named is a big overhang on the middle section some distance to the right of the route.

Start at the immediate edge of the buttress on the right of Amphitheatre Gully (cairn). Go up excellent rock for 6o feet to a belay below a quartz-studded nose. The buttress steepens. Move right and up over steep slabs then return horizontally to a balcony on the edge (thread). A fault in a slab slants up right to a small overhang which is climbed direct (M.S.). Move round a corner to the right then back left on easy slabs to the glacis below the middle section (2oo feet).

Above the glacis the bulge girdles the buttress. The problem is to reach the foot of a grass groove 4o feet up. To the left and below the groove on the very edge of the Gully is a pointed abutment. Vertical rock with good but widely spaced holds leads up this to a little ledge below a large overhang. The crux follows and is one of the hardest free pitches in the Cairngorms. The ledge slopes down very awkwardly to a little corner on the right where the vital holds necessary for pulling into the groove must be grasped quickly after an out-of-balance move. At the top of the groove there is a stance and belay on the left. A few feet higher traverse right to a slanting crack leading to easier ground. Trend back left by cracks towards the edge and end of middle section (200 feet).

The upper section gives easy but interesting climbing at one point passing a fine window. Near the top a steep little buttress gives a good finish starting by a crack a few feet up its right side (200 feet).

THE TENEMENTS   500 feet   VERY DIFFICULT

First ascent: G. H. Leslie, M. Smith and C. Petrie

August 14th 1955

To the right, the slabs of the Crag ease into a green gully which leads to a grassy amphitheatre. The Tenements lie on the right of this gully. A pleasant climb.

Start from a cairn and zig-zag up cracked slabs until the buttress steepens in a wall on the edge of the gully. Climb an awkward 20-foot corner on the right of the wall and traverse left to a perch on the edge (piton belay). Continue up the nose of slabs in front (M.S.) then gravitate naturally by grooves and little pitches to a prominent chimney high up. Climb the chimney which has a regular ladder of holds to easy ground. Round a corner to the left are huge overhangs, so move right and go up easy slabs to the top.

THE FLANKING CRAGS

STAC AN FHÀRAIDH OF CAIRNGORM

These are the glaciated, holdless slabs near the Saddle leading to Strath Nethy. One climb is recorded; at the left end where the smooth bolsters relent and a perfectly rectangular, low-walled rib comes down between a red gully on the left and the smooth slabs on the right.

RECTANGULAR RIB   270 feet   DIFFICULT

First ascent: J. Hansbury and W. Rae   *August 10th 1952*

At the start the walls of the rib are low and the first pitch is rather artificial. Higher up it is more interesting with two, fine, slab-pitches. Good slab-climbing.

Start at the foot and climb the initial slab in two steps for 25 feet then tackle the next slab by an upward traverse right ending in a holdless, upward movement on the right edge. Mainly pressure (V.D.). Start the next pitch at a small flake and again work right up a cracked slab to a point overlooking a chimney. A short step up to a platform. The rib ends here and the route goes up a hanging shelf. Work out to the left, then up heathery grooves to a second, smaller platform and evade the last grassy runnel by the rib on the left.

STACAN DUBHA OF BEINN MHEADHOIN

The crags to the left of the Beinn Mheadhoin–Cairn Etchachan col. From the Shelter Stone area they look quite imposing, but close inspection reveals discontinuity —what appears as one long ridge in profile is in actuality smaller ribs in different planes merging together. Two climbs are recorded which are also the longest. However, if length is not to be the sole criterion the remaining ribs and walls should give quite good climbs.

RIBBON RIDGE   350 feet   MODERATE

First ascent: T. W. Patey and A. Watson   *August 1st 1954*

At the eastern end of the crags immediately above a shoot of red scree almost reaching the lochside. It is situated between deep gullies. The rock requires a judicious handling. At the top there is an optional, difficult finish.

Indefinite slabby ground leads to the foot of the ridge (cairn). Climb a subsidiary rib on left, then traverse right and up a chimney to centre of ridge. A steep nose bars progress. The sporting way past this obstacle is a hand-traverse to the right across a slab. Easy to a tower. Beyond a small-scale "Tower Gap" follow the shelved crest till it abuts the upper wall. Here are easy escapes into the gully. A better and more difficult finish is had by traversing out to the left (D., exposed) till it becomes possible to go straight up, then return rightwards to gain an upper ridge close to the plateau.

THE SHUTTLE   300 feet   VERY DIFFICULT

First ascent: G. Adams and R. H. Sellers *April 7th 1957*

The highest and most prominent of the buttresses. Good rock and good climbing.

A detached lower section of cracked slabs gives a good introduction. On the main buttress climb a chimney on the right side to a terrace. The wall in front is very hard, so move up to the edge on the right. An awkward climb up woolsack rock leads on to the wall of the buttress— slabs dipping into the gully on the right. Traverse horizontally right above the gully then cut back to the crest by a chimney topped by a flake (M.S.). Climb smooth, shelving slabs to a short wall split by a crack. Easier climbing follows.

ON CREAG DHUBH, the crag one mile east of Stacan Dubha on the same mountain, there is one fairly good snow gully 400 feet high of Grade 1 standard, but no summer climbing.

THE NORTHERN CORRIES OF
CAIRNGORM AND BRAERIACH

THE great northern façade of the Cairngorms, unlike the southern front, is not hidden by intervening ridges, and from the Spey valley one looks over the sea of pines of Glenmore and Rothiemurchus to the heather uplands and high corries of Braeriach and Cairngorm, a scene epitomising the massif for most mountaineers and one in which the combination of forest and mountain scenery cannot be rivalled.

Of the five named corries which distinguish this aspect of Cairngorm, the westerly Coire an t-Sneachda and Coire an Lochain are the finest and only ones of interest to the rock-climber.

On Braeriach there are three northern corries: Coire Beanaidh, Coire Ruadh and Coire an Lochain. The climbing value of the first and second lies solely in their providing steep routes to the summit of the mountain in winter from Aviemore. In the steeper and more interesting Coire an Lochain there is good snow-climbing and one recorded rock-climb.

APPROACHES

1. To (*a*) *Coire an t-Sneachda* and (*b*) *Coire an Lochain of Cairngorm* from the Loch Morlich Y.H.—formerly Glenmore Lodge of the 1″ map (driving road from Aviemore).

(*a*) Follow the new motor road to Coire Cas and break off short of Jean's Hut to contour round the ridge separating the corries.

(*b*) Follow the motor road or old track and break off near the tree limit to cross a footbridge leading to

right side of the Allt Mor. Follow the track by the
Allt Creag an Leth-choin to its junction with the
stream issuing from Coire an Lochain, then follow
this.

2. **To** *the northern corries of Braeriach* from Aviemore.
The best approach is by Glen Einich to the site of the
Lower Bothy (bicycle or motor-bicycle), thence
follow the Beanaidh Bheag.

CAIRNGORM: COIRE AN T-SNEACHDA

Coire an t-Sneachda (pron. Trayach) is the easterly or
leftmost of the two rock-walled corries seen from Glenmore Lodge. It is separated from Coire an Lochain by
a long hump-backed ridge steepening to a fairly narrow
arête of rock leading to the summit plateau of Cairn
Lochan (3983 feet), the westerly top of Cairngorm. This
is the Fiacaill Coire an Lochain popularly known as the
Fiacaill Ridge. It is unnamed on the 1″ map and should
not be confused with the ridge named on that map as the
Fiacaill à Choire Chais which is on the opposite side of
the corrie.

Coire an t-Sneachda is deceptive in size. Viewed from
a distance it looks comparatively small but one enters it
to find a recess extending westward containing a fine
mass of rock buttressing the Fiacaill Ridge. This recess
is not seen from Loch Morlich Y.H.

There are four main rock masses. In the left hand
corner at the entrance is a high-lying buttress. On its
right flank is Jacob's Ladder, a steep gully. Aladdin
Buttress is in the centre of the corrie, its lower section
forming an imposing dome-shaped bastion. Aladdin's
Couloir curves round the left side of this mass. Between
Aladdin Buttress and the lowest point of the corrie rim is
the extensive Fluted Buttress seamed by many shallow

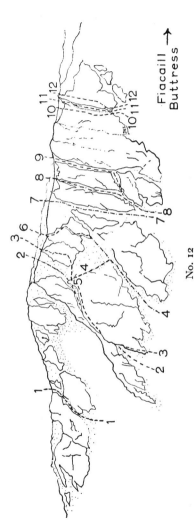

No. 12

CAIRNGORM: COIRE AN T-SNEACHDA

Fiacaill Buttress →

1—Jacob's Ladder   2—Aladdin's Couloir   3—Aladdin Buttress
4—Aladdin's Mirror   5—Aladdin's Seat   6—Pygmy Ridge   7—Central Gully
8—The Runnel   9—Crotched Gully   10—Fingers Ridge   11—Red Gully
12—Western Rib

gullies; gendarmes on its right skyline are known as the Fingers. Lastly in the westerly recess buttressing the Fiacaill Ridge is Fiacaill Buttress.

JACOB'S LADDER   250 feet   GRADE I

First ascent: A. Henderson and F. Mitchell   *Easter 1939*

A short winter route. There are long introductory snow slopes leading to the gully. There are no pitches under heavy snow, but there are steeper sections about a third of the way up, and again at the top. These are due to the snow overlying piled boulders in the gully bed.

ALADDIN'S COULOIR   500 feet   GRADE I

First ascent: A. Henderson and E. M. Davidson
March 24th 1935

Essentially a snow climb. The left bounding gully of Aladdin Buttress. Steep but straightforward. Following a confined initial section the gully opens out to the right and easy climbing leads to the top. The cornice will vary with conditions. Care required. In the event of a fall the party may be carried over Aladdin Buttress.

Aladdin Buttress

The most prominent buttress seen from Glenmore. Its main features are: (1) an imposing dome-shaped lower section culminating in easy ground leading to (2) a 30-foot pinnacle—Aladdin's Seat—and (3) two large triangular masses of rock in the upper section which from below look like large pinnacles breaking the skyline above and to the right of the Seat.

The climbs on the buttress are Original Route and the Lamp Direct, routes on the left side leading naturally to Aladdin's Seat and the leftmost triangular mass on the upper section. The right triangular mass whose position, definition and nature entitle it to be regarded as a separate climb, is Pygmy Ridge.

The prominent fault on the right flank of the lower section has been climbed, ascent being made partly in the fault, partly on the rib on the right (D. D. Stewart and R. Naylor, 1951), but the rib itself, climbed from its foot, is the better climb (D.) and makes for a sporting approach to Pygmy Ridge. Aladdin's Mirror starting on the extreme right of the lower section is purely a winter climb.

Some confusion has existed concerning the early winter ascents made here by S.M.C. parties in 1904, and it appears that the account in C.G. 1950 edition is incorrect in that Central Gully has been mistaken for Aladdin's Couloir. The mistakes have been rectified in the following descriptions of the routes.

ORIGINAL ROUTE   500 feet   VERY DIFFICULT
GRADE 4

First ascent: A. Henderson, E. M. Davidson, J. Geddes
    and A. Gray   *April 1936*
First winter ascent: T. W. Patey   *February 1959*

Start at the foot of Aladdin's Couloir up a slabby rib at the bottom left-hand corner of the buttress. Two good pitches, a wall and a groove lead to a spike belay at 80 feet. Go ahead for 100 feet on grass and rock to a belay (a slabby inclined ledge on the right marks the start of Lamp Direct) and continuing this line, climb a 20-foot pitch to a moss ledge. From the ledge at its left end go up a steep edge (V.D.) or alternatively a chimney on the right. Easy scrambling to Aladdin's Seat which is moderate.

One can now move into the Couloir but the natural

continuation is up the left-hand triangular mass which provides a hard finish even by its easiest line. Start up an open chimney 20 feet right of the left-hand corner of the tower and climb the left wall on small holds for 30 feet to a mossy slab crowned with overhangs. Move to the left then back right across the slab to a wall (delicate), then mantelshelf on to a ledge. The final pitch of 30 feet leads directly to the top. (Severe. Possibly G. McLeod, J. Henderson, I. Blake, R. Frost; August 1956.) No direct ascent up the left-hand corner has been recorded, although attempts have been made.

Variation: At the spike-belay 80 feet from start on lower section there is an obvious traverse out right under an overhang. Loose at the start, it improves with progress and after a chokestone-belay in a crack at 80 feet it is possible to climb up over a series of blocks to gain the crest. (Difficult. G. McLeod, J. Henderson, I. Blake, R. Frost; August 1956.)

Winter: No record of ascent by Original Route. First ascent by the conspicuous fault or gully on right flank. This provided two vertical ice-pitches climbed almost directly with slight deviations on to slabs on the left. Both pitches were very severe.

THE LAMP DIRECT   SEVERE

First ascent: R. Naylor and M. W. Parkin *August 9th 1953*

A variation on sound rock on the steep edge to the right of Original Route. There is an exposed pitch of 70 feet.

Follow Original Route for 180 feet. Now cross the overhanging wall on the right by a slabby, inclined ledge and traverse 15 feet beneath an overhang to a block, then return left on a sloping ledge below another overhang—two very delicate steps (S.). Continue up-

wards to a pile of blocks. Easy scrambling to Aladdin's
Seat (The Lamp).

ALADDIN'S MIRROR   500 feet   GRADE I

First ascent: An E.U.M.C. party   *1946*

A winter climb only. Rather indirect. Follow the
snow shelf, striking right from the lowest rocks of Aladdin
Buttress, then double back left up the first open gully
beyond the big fault on the right side of the buttress.
The gully debouches on steep snow below the upper
rocks. Traverse to the Seat and finish by Aladdin's
Couloir. Care required.

PYGMY RIDGE   250 feet   MODERATE

First ascent: H. Raeburn, W. A. Garden, G. H. Almond
  and —. Roth   *April 1st 1904*

The right-hand triangular mass on the upper section
of Aladdin Buttress. A good training climb on steep,
sound, moderate rock. The climbing is up a defined rib
which at one point forms a broken, level arête. The start
is cairned; the route obvious and enjoyable overlooking
Central Gully.

Fluted Buttress

The cliff face west of Aladdin Buttress to the lowest
point of the corrie rim is Fluted Buttress. A recessed
section next to Aladdin Buttress is furrowed by the
Trident gullies; Central Gully, The Runnel and
Crotched Gully. In winter these are most prominent
and extend upwards from a tapering snowfield. They
are not summer climbs. The ribs between the gullies
have little importance but one gives a good scramble.

On the right Fluted Buttress terminates in more

K

massive rocks and on the crest forming the skyline are the pinnacles known as the Fingers.

CENTRAL GULLY   300 feet   GRADE 1

First ascent: T. E. Goodeve, A. W. Russell and A. E.
    Robertson   *April 1st 1904*

The gully separating Aladdin from Fluted Buttress going up under the right side of Pygmy Ridge. A straightforward winter climb. It is less steep than the other gullies of the Trident and has no pitches. Often carries a good but easily outflanked cornice at its wide exit.

THE RUNNEL   300 feet   GRADE 2

First ascent: An E.U.M.C. party   *1946*

The central and best-defined gully of the Trident running directly down to the westerly of several lochans on the corrie floor. High-angled but quite straightforward to within 120 feet from the top where it forks. The left fork gives good climbing in a narrow chimney (perhaps 60 feet early in the season) leading to the final slope. Often heavily corniced.

The rib to the left of the Runnel is narrow and defined but is nowhere more than a simple scramble (J. B. Nimlin and D. Easson under heavy snow, March 1947).

CROTCHED GULLY   300 feet   GRADE 1

First ascent: An E.U.M.C. party   *1946*

The rightmost and least defined of the Trident gullies. Sometimes has a narrow, steep section leading right, from the snowfield into the main gully. Otherwise straightforward when the build-up is heavy.

BETWEEN Crotched Gully and the lowest point of the corrie rim the rocks become more massive. Here on the right side is the Red Gully bounded on its left by the pinnacled Fingers Ridge and on its right by Western Rib.

FINGERS RIDGE   350 feet   DIFFICULT

First ascent: D. Bennet   *September 1954*

Start at the foot of Red Gully (cairn). Climb up and to the left over slabs to some grass ledges (belays). Good climbing now follows. Climb nearly straight up on steep, open rock and then go slightly right to the foot of some slabs. Climb a groove on left of slabs to reach a narrow ridge. Follow the ridge over the Fingers and gain the plateau by a short wall.

RED GULLY   350 feet   GRADE 2

First ascent: Doubtful

A good winter gully. A better climb than the gullies of the Trident. Early in the season it twists up steeply between outcrops and often contains ice in quantity.

WESTERN RIB   300 feet   MODERATE

First ascent: D. Bennet   *April 1957*

A most prominent toadstool pinnacle lies at the foot of the rib on the right of Red Gully. Its top is guarded by steep rock. Climb the Red Gully and traverse on to the rib just above the pinnacle. Follow rib which is steep and narrow initially then easy over blocks to a tower climbed by cracks on its left. A short ridge connects the tower to the plateau. Slightly artificial because of grass strips on the right but a pleasant route nevertheless.

STANDING aloof in the western sector of the cirque and buttressing the upper part of the Fiacaill Ridge is a fine mass of rock 400 feet high. This is Fiacaill Buttress. Bounding the buttress on its right is Fiacaill Couloir, a curving gully.

FIACAILL BUTTRESS   400 feet   DIFFICULT

First ascent: W. Rae and J. Hansbury   *August 12th 1952*

The route is on the obvious rib just left of Fiacaill Couloir.

Climb the lowest rocks by a moss-grown groove. The rib is now indefinite for some way and the route lies on the edge of the Couloir. When the rib steepens move slightly left well on to the rib and climb a few steep pitches to the foot of a tower with a smooth wall. The wall has been climbed and is severe (G. McLeod, 1956) but it is readily evaded by an easy descending traverse to the left whence a chimney with good flake holds leads to easy ground and scrambling to the top of the tower. Beyond the tower cross a narrow col at the top of the Couloir. There is a final pitch to the top.

FIACAILL COULOIR   400 feet   GRADE 3

First ascent: T. W. Patey   *January 17th 1958*

The best of the winter gullies in the corrie. Will usually have much ice early in the season. Later it may bank out and become easier. On the first ascent in good conditions the main difficulties were a 20-foot ice-pitch at the start and the last pitch before the neck at the top of the buttress. Here the gully is blocked by an over-hang, but this was overcome by means of a good snow take-off. In between there were several minor ice-pitches of interest.

FIACAILL RIDGE

EASY

A simple rock scramble if the ridge is adhered to strictly throughout. The most direct way to the summit of Cairn Lochan from Glenmore. Under heavy snow it is most sporting and enjoyable.

CAIRNGORM: COIRE AN LOCHAIN

Whereas Coire an t-Sneachda is open and its rock wall discontinuous, Coire an Lochain is confined and its cliff continuity unbroken.

The outstanding feature of the corrie is a great 350-foot slab of bare, red granite rising above the main lochan and forming a curious apron to the encircling buttresses. It is inclined at a moderate angle and is conspicuous from Speyside where the reflected light from its damp surface is often mistaken for snow.

Avalanches of really big dimensions occur on the slab in thaw conditions in winter and spring and have to be guarded against. The break usually occurs near the top of the slab when snow perhaps 10–15 feet in depth sloughs off clean and slides in huge blocks to the lochan leaving high marginal fracture-walls reminiscent of glacier scenery.

There are four major buttresses encircling the slab. On the extreme left No. 1 Buttress shows up as a vertical wall cut by ledges and cracks. Hard under the wall of No. 1 Buttress is the Vent, a conspicuous narrow gully, short, with one chokestone. Between the Vent and the Couloir (the next gully near the cliff-centre) rises the recessed wall of No. 2 Buttress with Central Crack route on its right flank. Ewen or No. 3 Buttress, having more of the true buttress form, bounds the right side of the Couloir. Another recess split by a steep pillar cuts back

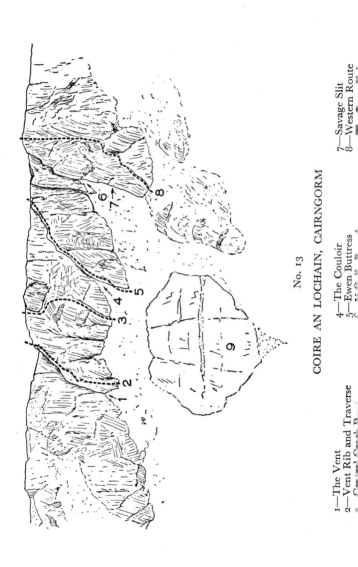

No. 13

COIRE AN LOCHAIN, CAIRNGORM

1—The Vent
2—Vent Rib and Traverse
3—Central Crack Route

4—The Couloir
5—Ewen Buttress

7—Savage Slit
8—Western Route

into the cliff right of Ewen Buttress. Two gullies separated by the pillar are the Left and Right Branches of Y gully. Finally on the right side of the corrie over-hanging the lochan is No. 4 Buttress, very steep on its left flank where it harbours a fine route—Savage Slit.

The buttresses though not high (max. 350 feet) are impressive but the inner two hold much vegetation and shattered rock. It is perhaps unfortunate that, because of their location and standard, these buttresses have become popular amongst instructor-led parties on climb-ing courses. It is to be hoped that no false impression of granite will be engendered in the minds of trainees by these climbs. Savage Slit on No. 4 Buttress, however, more than makes good these blemishes. It is a first-rate climb and one of the best in the massif.

Criticisms of the corrie under summer conditions are naturally nullified by the snow and ice of winter. Then it gives excellent climbing.

The climbs, left to right, are:

No. 1 BUTTRESS

On the extreme left of the corrie. Shows up as a vertical wall easing to broken ground on its left flank. It is split by many cracks. Direct ascents have been attempted but the promising lines have petered out and all parties have diverged to the easy ground on the left.

THE VENT   350 feet   SEVERE.   GRADE 2–3

First ascent (winter): E. M. Davidson, R. F. Stobart, Miss
          Macbain and J. Geddes   *April 13th 1935*
First summer ascent: F. F. Cunningham and A. G. Mac-
          Kenzie   *October 30th 1948*

The prominent, short gully between the wall of No. 1 Buttress and an offshoot rib of No. 2 Buttress. It runs up to the summit of Cairn Lochan and is very wet in all weathers.

After an initial 20-foot step easy climbing leads to a cave below a large chokestone. Overcome this by backing up, or if lacking in inches climb the left wall (S.). Another easier chokestone follows.

Winter: Difficulties depend on the bank-up of snow at the first chokestone which usually forms a high ice-draped pitch in early season. Moderately-angled above to cornice. (M.M.C.J. 1.45.)

VENT RIB AND TRAVERSE   350 feet   DIFFICULT

First ascent: H. Watt and W. A. Russell *September 4th 1949*

The attractive flying ridge of No. 2 Buttress bounding the right bank of the Vent is Vent Rib. Some distance up this becomes very steep and smooth and this section is circumvented by a long traverse.

Climb the rib for 150 feet to an overhang. Above, the arête is steep and smooth. Escape to the right across a chimney below the overhang and make a prolonged traverse across the wall on the right round a shattered corner to a flake (90 feet). Now go up behind a block to a delightful slant across a slab to easy ground.

No. 2 Buttress

This is recessed in its centre between Vent Rib and the right flank which steepens as it rounds into the Couloir. The right flank is topped by a conspicuous, steep square-cut wall which the sole recorded route on the buttress avoids by a left traverse. This is Central Crack Route, named by the pioneers, not for its position on the buttress but for its being the natural continuation of a crack up the centre of the great slab which they followed to gain the buttress. The great slab, however, by its centre line is a scramble only and does not merit description.

Steeper routes might be made on either side of Central Crack Route but no guarantee can be given as to the integrity of the rock.

CENTRAL CRACK ROUTE   350 feet
MODERATE. GRADE 3

First ascent: A. Harrison and L. St. C. Bartholomew
July 1931
First winter ascent: T. W. Patey   *February 2nd 1958*

Popular but undeservedly so. There is loose rock, vegetation and sandy ledges.

Start above a bright green moss-patch below the entrance to the Couloir up a well-defined crack slanting slightly right. The first pitch (avoided by the pioneers on the right) is 20 feet and difficult. The second is a short chimney followed by easier climbing. Now move left following a crack to a poised, square block which can be climbed over or through. The route is now obvious; mainly scrambling but there are two short pitches. Slant round to the left of the great square wall. (J. 19.244–246.)

The ferocious crack cutting the face of the square wall has been climbed (70 feet, V.S.)—G. J. Dewar, C. Allen and D. Knight. *August 1959.*

Winter: An interesting climb and because of its recessed position often holding snow when the other faces are free. The first two pitches may present considerable difficulty if heavily iced. Thereafter the climbing while quite exposed should not be too hard. There are several alternatives on the upper section, but the easiest line is awkward to find.

THE wide corridor separating No. 2 Buttress from Ewen or No. 3 Buttress is "The Couloir".

THE COULOIR   350 feet   EASY. GRADE 1

First descent (winter): E. M. Davidson and A. Henderson
March 24th 1935

Loose and moss grown. Most of the unpleasantness can be avoided by scrambling up a rib in the centre. Not a good means of descent in summer.

Winter: A uniform 45° slope fairly heavily corniced. The easiest winter climb in the corrie.

EWEN BUTTRESS (No. 3 BUTTRESS)   350 feet
MODERATE. GRADE 3

First ascent: J. Ewen, E. M. Davidson and T. Davidson
April 23rd 1933
First winter ascent: T. W. Patey and V. N. Stevenson
February 1959

The best defined of the buttresses; ridge-like in form standing out between the Couloir and the recess holding the Y Gully Branches. The right flank is very steep. The buttress was named by the M.M.C. in memory of their member John Ewen who was killed in the Alps.

From the foot of the Couloir climb steep but broken rock for 130 feet to a saddle. The face above is cut in the middle by an open gully. Climb the gully until a pitch bars the way. Take the crack on the right then scramble to the short (40 feet) final face. Above, the buttress is linked to the plateau by a narrow neck.

Winter: Though short its upper narrow section makes this an interesting and worthwhile climb, especially under heavy snow. Entry into the open gully above the saddle may provide the hardest move.

A VERY steep pillar is the main feature of the recess biting far back into the plateau to the right of Ewen Buttress. The pillar rises between two gullies—the so-called Branches of Y Gully. The pillar is unclimbed and the Branches winter climbs only.

LEFT BRANCH Y GULLY   350 feet   GRADE 3

First ascent: T. W. Patey, A. G. Nicol and A. Wedderburn
November 16th 1952

Difficulty depends on quantity of ice present. On the first ascent it carried a 20-foot ice-pitch which was rather hard. With alternate thaw and freeze over a long period it may present more continuous ice and difficulty late in the season.

RIGHT BRANCH Y GULLY   350 feet   GRADE 2

First ascent: R. F. Stobart, T. Stobart, Miss Harbinson and E. M. R. Thompstone   *April 14th 1934*

Straightforward but high-angled. Requires good, hard snow. The cornice may be large and unbroken, giving a difficult finish (M.M.C.J. 1.36).

No. 4 Buttress

The squat crag on the right of the corrie above the main lochan. It is very steep on its left and centre gradually easing on its right to more broken ground below a series of open gullies set between small, upper buttresses.

Hidden from view on its left flank is Savage Slit, a narrow crack set into a vertical, right-angled corner. Western Route slants from the left of the north-facing rocks then diverges right to easier ground and finishes by one of the small gullies in the upper buttress.

Sounder rock here than elsewhere in the corrie.

SAVAGE SLIT   350 feet   VERY DIFFICULT. GRADE 4

First ascent: R. B. Frere and J. D. Walker *July 17th 1945*
First winter ascent: G. Adams, J. White and F. Henderson
April 21st 1957

A remarkable route up a narrow fissure formed by the vertical jointing of the granite. By far the best route in the corrie and among the best in the massif—sound, clean rock and fine situations.

Go round the foot of the buttress by a terrace above some broken rock into the recess holding the Y Gully Branches. The Slit can now be seen cleaving the wall of the buttress.

Climb a moderate 30-foot pitch to the foot of the actual fissure. The initial 20 feet in the crack up to and over a chokestone is fairly strenuous. The crack now goes far into the buttress and progress is easy for 15 feet inwards. Now gain a jammed chokestone by an outward traverse. The next pitch of 50 feet is exposed; climb on the very edge of the crack on small holds to another large chokestone. Pass the boulder on the outside. The crack can now be followed out to the top (80 feet) but it is worth-while climbing the horizontally creased wall on the right for the exposed situation (M.). The crack ends in a gap in the buttress forming a pinnacle. Continue up the broken buttress. (J. 23.349.)

Winter: Found very hard even in the rather favourable conditions prevailing (after fresh snow near the end of a season of less than average snowfall). The introductory rocks, powder-covered, were easy. The Slit itself between chokestones was blocked out partially with old ice, partially with packed powder. The upper chokestones provided the hardest moves. These were heavily iced and the walls of the Slit sheathed in verglas. One rock-piton used at each; at the first for a runner, at the second (crux) for direct aid on an extremely hard move out of the crack. Time: $3\frac{1}{2}$ hours.

WESTERN ROUTE   400 feet
VERY DIFFICULT. GRADE 3

First ascent: C. Ross, J. Brewster and D. Banks *May 1949*
First winter ascent: T. W. Patey   *February 1959*

Up the north-facing rocks starting from a cairn near the centre. Go along a difficult crack and a ledge slanting right to a platform in 70 feet. A short pitch now leads to a grass recess with a blank wall of 20 feet barring progress. This is the crux. Employ combined tactics. Still technically severe—a nice problem confronts the unfortunate last man. Follow a chimney with smooth V walls for 50 feet to easier climbing leading to the prominent final gully (wide chimney) to the left of a small, steep upper buttress. Avoid the overhang at the gully top on the right.

Winter: This is a climb with sustained difficulty in genuine conditions. On the first ascent there were several severe pitches, the hardest being the chimney above the summer crux. The wall of the summer crux itself was banked with snow and went relatively easily.

LESSER ROCKS

There are short recognised routes in the defile of Creag a Chalamain and on the outcrop of rock (Cranberry Rocks) at the outlet of Coire na Ciste on its east side which are used as practice climbs by S.C.P.R. students at Glenmore. Though containing many excellent little pitches these routes cannot be detailed.

BRAERIACH: COIRE AN LOCHAIN

This is the rightmost of the triune of corries which gives Braeriach its fine character as seen from Speyside. It is the most interesting scenically of the three and the only one having rock for climbing. The loch from which it derives its name is the finest specimen of mountain tarn in the Cairngorms and the largest sheet of water at such an elevation (3267 feet) in the country.

The loch is girt by slabs but the only defined climb is on the right side where a pinnacled ridge rises on the right of a narrow gully.

DERELICT RIDGE   270 feet   DIFFICULT

First ascent: R. B. Frere and P. A. Densham   *June 1945*

The most sporting as well as the shortest way from Glen Einich to the summit of Braeriach.

The ridge is very steep on its acute edge overlooking the gully and near the top forms a pinnacle. Good climbing up moderate slabs formed in steps on the right side followed by steeper rock giving a difficult pitch leads to the top of the pinnacle. Beyond a break another steep pitch leads to the flat top of an upper tower.

The narrow gully on the left of the ridge has been climbed many times in winter. Though short it gives a good straightforward climb—the best defined in the corrie.

COIRE RUADH, the central of the three corries, gives fair snow-climbing and the narrow ridges bounding it on either side are interesting winter routes to the plateau. That on the left forming the boundary with Coire Beanaidh and leading direct to the summit of Braeriach being the best.

CLIMBS IN THE DEFILE OF THE LAIRIG GHRU

THESE are situated on the crags of Sròn na Lairig (3875 feet), the northern top of Braeriach, and on the ribs ascending to the pointed summit of Creag an Leth-choin (The Lurcher's Crag, 3448 feet), the westerly, outlying top of Cairngorm.

The crags, with the exception of one climb on Sròn na Lairig, have little attraction, but in their opposing each other in the defile at its narrowest portion they contribute greatly to the character of what is probably the grandest mountain pass in the country.

SRÒN NA LAIRIG

At the north end of the crag here, long, steep slab-edges would give fair climbs but lacking in character. The best feature of the crag is a fine, towered ridge at the southern or summit end. This is Lairig Ridge, the longest and best climb from the pass.

LAIRIG RIDGE   450 feet   DIFFICULT

First ascent: W. D. Brooker and T. Shaw *July 7th 1950*

An exhilarating climb on grand rock. The most sporting route to the summit of Braeriach from Glenmore.

Straddling its base is a great slabby wall 100 feet high. Climb the wall by its right edge. Traverse left at the top to avoid an overhang then climb a short wall to easy ground. Scrambling for 100 feet leads to the ridge proper. Start on this up to the right by a steep wall then slabs to a short chimney leading to the crest (50 feet). Follow crest directly, over a series of towers interspersed with vertical walls and knife-edges. Near the top the ridge levels out.

The rib forming the right-hand border of the section holding the Ridge has also been climbed but it is a poor route.

CREAG AN LETH-CHOIN
(LURCHER'S CRAG)

The line of ribs is divided into three sections, Southern, Central and Northern, by the easy North and South gullies. The Central section rises to the summit of Creag an Leth-choin. The ribs are shortest but at their most defined in the Southern section opposite Lairig Ridge.

In preparation for this guide the most attractive routes were climbed. None gave climbing of more than moderate difficulty, but since the rock is sound, holds most satisfying and anchorages plentiful they should provide good practice for beginners.

Southern Section. Southern Ridge is the best route on the crag. Longest in its section and the first defined climb as seen approaching from the Pools of Dee. From the lowest rocks climb steep but easy rock to reach a chimney just right of two prominent boulders 150 feet up. Thence easy scrambling to the top of a tower. From the col behind, climb a steep chimney to the left of the actual crest for 60 feet. Easier climbing follows. (400 feet. Moderate.)

In the centre of the section and to the left of Southern Ridge is a large grass recess at the back of which rises a prominent dark chimney. Two ribs bound the recess diverging from each other as they rise. Both ribs were climbed. That on the left is narrow and short, rising in a series of abrupt steps (200 feet. Moderate). That on the right follows a slanting course to the right of a grassy chimney (300 feet. Moderate).

The indeterminate ridge to the right of the South Gully was descended. Near the top is a small pinnacle seen to best advantage from further up the Lairig Ghru track. (300 feet. Moderate.)

Central and Northern Sections. Here the rocks are for the most part indeterminate but the buttress on the North Section bordering North Gully gives a fair climb. The start is on top of the rubbly ridge forming the bank of the gully where it meets the buttress. There are three good, short pitches then the climb degenerates into a ridge walk. (300 feet. Moderate. Philpott, Wylie, Gregory; 1951.)

L

THE GREAT AMPHITHEATRE OF
BRAERIACH (4248 feet) AND
CAIRNTOUL (4241 feet)

CAIRNTOUL, shapeliest yet the least interesting of the greater Cairngorm summits, is honoured in sharing with Braeriach (in its infinite variety one of the most fascinating mountains in the country) a giant arena of corries drained by the headwaters of the River Dee. Stretching two miles across from summit to summit with a rim edging the plateau for nearly four miles, this cirque is in its magnitude without parallel in these islands. It is also the most alpine of our mountain areas in point of snow-accumulation and the prolonged period of its cover—conditions resulting from a combination of factors. Chief of these is topography; for all but two of the corries lie under the great plateau of Braeriach in the lee of the prevailing winds; and the plateau—itself a vast collecting area—is further backed by a gently sloping tableland extending west to An Moine Mhòr (The Great Moss) above Glen Feshie. From this extensive desert of snow, drift is carried by the wind for many miles and finally driven into the corries where it piles to great depths.

Another singular and magnificent feature of the cirque is the formation in certain years of the longest, unbroken cornice found on our mountains. At peak season it reaches giant proportions over many sections on its four-mile circuit.

Snow in such quantity and permanence gives the area an added attraction in summer, for the snowiest and best corries for climbing are open to the sun. It is strongly recommended therefore that the area should be visited for summer climbing in early June. Then the buttresses, bare of snow and separated by corniced gullies, rise from unbroken snowfields and the whole scene creates an atmosphere which is truly Alpine.

The corries in clockwise succession from Cairntoul are:
1. Coire an Lochain Uaine.
2. Corrie of the Chokestone Gully.
3. Garbh Choire Mòr.
4. Garbh Choire Dhàidh.   } An Garbh Choire.
5. Coire Bhrochain.

APPROACHES

The best base is Corrour Bothy in Glen Dee (Derry Lodge, 5½ miles). From Corrour keep high on the west side of the Dee to the moraines at the headwater junction. Avoid the moraines and drop to the Allt a Garbh Choire to hug its left bank. The best way now to An Garbh Choire is obvious. For Coire Bhrochain it is advised not to slant up too quickly—cross the Allt a Garbh Choire opposite the stream issuing from the lip of the corrie and follow this. (Coire Bhrochain, 2 hours; An Garbh Choire recesses, 2½ hours.)

An alternative route, quicker but more strenuous, to An Garbh Choire is recommended, but in summer only, and in clear weather. From Corrour go up the path in Coire Odhar, then up to the rim of Coire an t-Saighdeir. From here contour Cairntoul and Sgòr an Lochain Uaine without losing height and descend into Garbh Choire Mòr by broken slopes east of the Braeriach–Cairntoul col.

CAMP SITES AND BIVOUAC

The area being remote, a base nearer the cliffs may be preferred. There are good sites on the Dee flats about two miles from Corrour and at various points upstream from here. Garbh Choire Dhàidh is recommended if a camp in the corries is planned—there is a delectable site on a large area of the finest turf bordering the Dee where it opens out into small pools beyond the lip of the corrie. Just above the pools is the Dey-Smith Bivouac, a built-up cave under the second largest boulder. It is the only shelter in a great area and holds two comfortably. It should be noted in case of emergency.

COIRE AN LOCHAIN UAINE

The symmetrical hanging corrie between the peaks of Cairntoul and Sgòr an Lochain Uaine (Angel's Peak).

Harbouring short mouldering arêtes and uninteresting slabs only, it is of little importance to the climber in summer. It improves with the snow of winter and is steep enough all round to provide fair sport. The best climbs then are the North-East Ridge of Sgòr an Lochain Uaine on the edge of the corrie leading directly to its summit (easy, but interesting, especially near the top, where it narrows) and the long slopes on the immediate left of the ridge which run up steeply for 1000 feet from the loch to the corniced summit edge.

CORRIE OF THE CHOKESTONE GULLY (SGÒR AN LOCHAIN UAINE)

For some distance west of its North-East Ridge the rocks of Sgòr an Lochain Uaine flanking the valley are ill-defined though continuous and steep low down. Near the entrance to Garbh Choire Mòr they recede upwards to form the headwall of a high corrie or bay, usually accepted as being part of Garbh Choire Mòr but so well-defined as to merit distinction. Through usage it has been named after its well-known and unmistakable feature—a dark, twisting gash cleaving the steepest rocks. Two climbs only are recorded, but there is scope for exploration.

CHOKESTONE GULLY   500 feet
           MODERATE. GRADE 3

First ascent: J. McCoss and G. Merchant
                                September 25th 1911
First winter ascent: A. H. Hendry and party *March 1937*

A first-rate winter climb; rather grimy in summer. The gully bed, carved in the solid rock, is wet and mossy. A series of boulder pitches providing short steps leads to the final great chokestone. This can be overcome directly in the right corner by a wet chimney (S. Tewnion, 1941. V.D.) or the pitch evaded entirely by climbing the right wall (25 feet).

Winter: For 200 feet the gully is straightforward though high-angled, then it curves, narrows and steepens to what is usually a long snow-ice pitch. Beyond this and above a snow amphitheatre is a high, vertical ice-fall— the great chokestone. Difficulty here will depend on the time of visit and the snow build-up. On the first ascent (in one of the great snow years) there was only a short vertical step. On the second (1954) the pitch was 25 feet in height. The exit is steep and the cornice heavy all round, but easier on the right. Time on second ascent: 3½ hours.

BUGABOO RIB   500 feet   VERY SEVERE (V.)

First ascent: R. W. P. Barclay, C. Annand, M. Smith and
    D. Steele   *July 1958*

The buttress bounding the right flank of Chokestone Gully and tapering to a ridge above its lower, steep section. The start lies between the centre line and the gully.

Climb easy slabby rocks for 40 feet to a grass platform. A slanting crack on the vertical wall ahead leads up right to a prominent block. Climb the crack (out of balance and poor holds) for 20 feet, traverse round the block and under an overhang then continue straight up to a large platform (90 feet). Climb another crack leading right (strenuous) up to a landing place under an overhang (40 feet), then move round the exposed corner to the right (awkward with hidden holds) and continue along a tapering shelf to a belay. Above this the ridge falls back and it is an easy scramble up to more respectable rocks at the top.

AN GARBH CHOIRE OF BRAERIACH

The great hollow forming the innermost recesses of the Amphitheatre—perhaps the most intriguing corrie in the massif on account of size, remoteness, wildness allied to beauty, and above all climate. Here are found the snowfields of midsummer—our nearest approach in this country to the névé of higher mountains.

A large headland thrusting out from the plateau divides the corrie into two subsidiaries, each of great interest and character. These are Garbh Choire Mòr and Garbh Choire Dhàidh. Their cliffs are the least known in the massif—a situation at once disappointing yet delighting their devotees.

GARBH CHOIRE MÒR

The left-hand and larger subsidiary. It has two sections; a lower corrie or entrance hall leading to an upper recessed pocket of buttresses tucked high under the plateau.

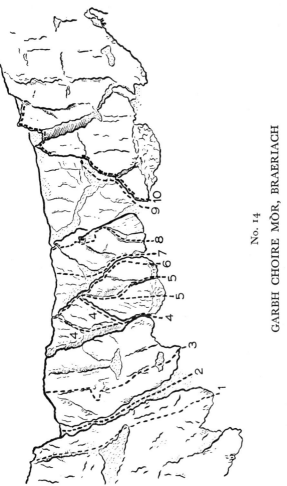

No. 14

GARBH CHOIRE MÒR, BRAERIACH

1—Crown Buttress
2—Great Gully
3—She-Devil's Buttress
4—Bunting's Gully

5—Michaelmas Fare
6—Egyptian Fantasy
7—Solo Gully

8—Sphinx Ridge
9—Pinnacle Gully
10—Pinnacles Buttress

THE LOWER CORRIE

The rocks here are somewhat indefinite though the scarp from the Corrie of the Chokestone Gully westward is continuous. There are three named features: Col Gully, the prominent scree rake going up to the Cairntoul-Braeriach col (*c.* 3700 feet); West Buttress on the immediate right of the gully, rather broken but with an interesting 180 foot pillar on its lower right flank (an entertaining V.D.—R. H. Sellers, G. Annand, M. Smith, 1957); and West Gully, a long shoot separating West Buttress from the buttresses of the upper corrie.

In winter much is wiped out but the gullies give fair Grade 1 climbs. Col Gully though well corniced is short and open. West Gully, longer, steeper and often heavily corniced, is the better climb.

THE UPPER CORRIE

The buttresses are mainly narrow and compact, not lending themselves to variation. Their rock is rather smooth though not unaccommodating on the established routes. It bears a patina of lichen which apparently thrives on granite covered for long periods by snow and is responsible for the remarkable, greenish hue of the buttresses which is most pronounced when they are seen in contrast with the snowfield and gullies. Although the rock is sound, extensive shattering occurs in places at the plateau. Care should be exercised in rope-management.

The cliff is not fully worked out in summer and some problems remain. In winter it is practically untouched and will repay those with initiative and time.

Snow: Due primarily to its location the upper corrie is unique in Britain for its annual accumulation of snow and as the site of our most permanent snow-beds; within living memory these have only disappeared in the years 1933 and 1959.

At peak conditions narrow gullies are transformed into open snow slopes and many rock features are wiped out.

The main buttresses, due to the build-up at their bases (estimated 100 feet in a heavy year in one case) and the spread of the gullies, are greatly diminished in height and breadth. For these reasons identification may be difficult in thick weather.

The cornice, which is without a flaw, reaches giant proportions (35 feet in height over one long section) and provides otherwise easy climbs with problematical finishes.

Certain peculiarities found in summer should be noted: (a) The cornice may be unbroken in June. (b) The gullies may not be clear at the end of July. (c) The snowfield under the cliffs will remain unbroken in a good year through August (in an average year in July it extends the width of the corrie and is 300 feet in height, steep, and, under the melt layer, icy). (d) Schrunds can be awkward and true crevasses open up below the innermost buttresses.

Another interesting feature is the formation on the north wall of the corrie (where there is a most beautiful and regular curtain of snow) of ice-grottoes and tunnels below the plateau after the fall of the cornices.

The climbs from left to right:

CROWN BUTTRESS   400 feet   VERY DIFFICULT

First ascent: K. Winram, C. Petrie, M. Smith and J.
    Tewnion   *August 13th 1950*

The large mass separating the lower from the upper corrie. Its left flank is broken by a broad scree-grass terrace above and below which are steep walls. On its right flank (in the upper corrie proper) it forms a continuous arête from which vertical walls dip into Great

Gully. The Crown—a flake of rock—can be seen against the sky at the top of the arête.

Start on the immediate edge of Great Gully (cairn). Follow smooth granite ribs to a large block climbed by a crack on the left. Step right and climb into a groove then scramble to the foot of the conspicuous chimney on the left of the arête. This gives a good, continuous 110-foot pitch. Climb by backing and jamming up to and over a culminating chokestone. Care required to the plateau from here.

GREAT GULLY   400 feet   EASY. GRADE I

First ascent: A. Tewnion and S. R. Tewnion   *July 1940*
First winter ascent: Uncertain

The most defined gully in the corrie but little more than a scramble in summer. It has three indefinite pitches and will often harbour one or more snow "plugs" throughout the year.

Winter: Straightforward but steep and heavily corniced.

SHE-DEVIL'S BUTTRESS   400 feet   VERY DIFFICULT

First ascent: K. Winram and M. Smith   *May 24th 1953*

The buttress forming the right wall of Great Gully and separated from an overhanging unclimbed buttress on its right by twin cracks. An interesting route with one very hard pitch.

Start at the foot of a long tail of slab-ribs bordering the gully. For 150 feet the going is easy but delightful up to a spearhead of rock set below two vicious high-angled slabs. At the top of the spearhead climb the left-hand crack on lower slab till it peters out overlooking Great Gully. Make a long delicate stride to the left and continue up easier rock to a crack separating the slabs. Climb the crack to a fine eyrie with table-top belay anchor. Climb the vertical wall in front (sketchy holds, V.D.) to the crest of the buttress and gain the plateau by slabs and grooves.

BUNTING'S GULLY   300 feet   MODERATE

First ascent: G. Dey, M. Smith, K. Winram and G. C. Greig   *July 22nd 1952*

The first prominent gully to the right of Great Gully. On its right are twin ridges separated low down by a huge recess but meeting 80 feet from the plateau at a col common to both. The gully forks at less than mid-height; the right fork runs up to the col of the twin ridges; the left fork ends in an overhanging chimney at the plateau. The chimney of the left branch has not been climbed.

The gully below the fork contains some choke-blocks which are easily passed. Entry to the right fork is by a little wall above which there are two easy pitches to the col.

A route to the plateau has been made using the left fork as far as the base of its final chimney: Beyond the junction a water-washed groove leads to a chokestone. Above this and at the foot of the chimney climb the right wall on steep rock, moderate but requiring care. (350 feet. Moderate. K. Winram and M. Smith, August 1953.)

MICHAELMAS FARE   350 feet   VERY DIFFICULT

First ascent: J. M. Taylor and G. B. Leslie
                                          September 29th 1954

This route is on the left-hand and most upright of the twin ridges to the right of Bunting's Gully. The left-hand ridge is separated from its crook-backed twin by a great slabby recess. The route followed starts in this recess and is not quite direct.

Go up the recess for 60 feet to a prominent open corner breaking the left wall. Climb the corner and the difficult step above it to the crest. Continue up the crest. When a vertical nose blocks the way traverse up the smooth slabs on the left which lead to the sneck or col common to both ridges. Straight ahead, steep but moderate rock for 80 feet leads to a section of shattered granite at the plateau.

Direct Start: A direct start to the ridge linking up with this route had been made on an earlier attempt; the climb being abandoned at the vertical nose due to bad weather: Start at the lowest rocks (covered for most of the year). Climb and cross narrow slab-ribs and their attendant grooves on a rightward trend to gain the crest above the open corner leading from the recess. The ribs are smooth, continuous and deceptively difficult. (Very difficult. K. Winram, G. C. Greig and M. Smith; July 1952.)

EGYPTIAN FANTASY   350 feet   DIFFICULT

First ascent: K. Winram and C. Petrie: G. C. Greig and
     M. Smith   *June 14th 1953*

The crook-backed twin. Its left side angles into the recess; its right forms a crest overlooking Solo Gully, a narrow groove in its lower part, opening out into a shallow depression at less than mid-height.

Start mid-way between the recess and Solo Gully. Go up a series of cracks on steep slabs for about 50 feet then make a right traverse and an upward exposed move which leads to the crest. The crest forms a series of easy steps to a platform of piled blocks below a vertical wall at the head of the recess.

The direct and aesthetic way from here is to climb a crack in the middle of the wall, gained by an upward left traverse and a delicate stride (M.S.) after which the crest continues easily to the col. The easiest route from the platform to the col is to traverse into Solo Gully from which it can be reached over broken rock. From the col to the plateau the route is that of Michaelmas Fare.

SOLO GULLY   300 feet   DIFFICULT

First ascent: A. Tewnion   *July 1941*

This starts as a narrow V groove which is followed by a section containing a series of chokestones some of which are awkward to pass. After this promising start the gully widens and becomes loose and scree-filled. Beyond the fork to the col of Egyptian Fantasy the true continuation of the gully is entered by a mossy groove above which there are messy slabs only.

Winter: The cliff between Great Gully and Solo Gully is untouched in winter. Something might be written of the easier possibilities.

Solo Gully, the easiest proposition, should provide a straightforward climb but as the particular section in which it lies boasts the biggest cornice in the Cairngorms (in some years 35 feet in height to the right of the chimney of Bunting's Gully) it should always provide a difficult finish. Bunting's Gully by its right fork is also straightforward to its col but from here steep, tapering arêtes swing up to giant cornices. Another route which should give a first-rate climb is the rightmost of the twin chimney-cracks between She-Devil's Buttress and its unclimbed neighbour. In most years it harbours a series of ice pitches.

SPHINX RIDGE   300 feet   VERY DIFFICULT UP TO JULY

First ascent: K. Winram, G. Dey, M. Smith and W. Kelly
May 25th 1952

Situated at the innermost point of the corrie above the snowfield, the Ridge rises rather shapely between Solo Gully on its left and—according to the time of visit—either a wide section of slab or a great rock-fringed snow-recess on its right. It is the best defined rock structure in the corrie. It is also something of a curio; for as the snow gradually recedes from its base (average year build-up estimated 80 feet at peak) so a smooth nose is brought to light which has so far prevented ascent of the Ridge in the latter months of the year. This nose will usually make its appearance by the end of July.

The frontal face is vertical and curiously incised. On its left is a fault ending in an overhang. Cross the "randkluft", which may be wide, deep and awkward, mid-way between these features and climb a great slab which is the chamfered edge of the frontal face, on a rightward trend to a fine situation on the undercut crest (90-foot run-out in May). Follow a short knife-edge to a belay below a wall at the slab apex. Go through an awkward gap between the wall and a rock-tooth leaning over space and pull up to a platform below the slab-pedestal of the Sphinx. The Sphinx (uncommonly like a scaled-down Cioch a' Sgumain from here) has not been climbed directly. Go left round a corner and climb a mossy crack then awkward slabs to a narrow ridgeway broken by a col formed by gullies running up on either side of the Ridge. Climb a moss-grown wall to the foot of a long, steep recess on the right with an overhang in its left corner. Climb the recess to a gap above the over-hang by the slab on the right (small holds, V.D.) and gain the top of a pinnacle by easier rock. The plateau is reached by a short descent to a sneck and a rise over loose rock.

Winter: Though short, the Ridge should give a beautiful climb after heavy snow. Under these conditions, nobly isolated, it rises from snowfield to plateau cornice as a sinuous snow crest often double corniced at its ridgeway.

THE BROAD RECESS of indeterminate slabs lying between Sphinx Ridge and Pinnacles Buttress, the next major feature on the right, is rather uninteresting in summer but three routes are recorded. Gullies run up the margins of the recess close into the bounding ridge and buttress. That under Sphinx is indefinite, has one big pitch and is unnamed (A. Watson and P. D. Baird; October 1954). The other is Pinnacle Gully. A moderate route has also been made up the slabs starting close to Pinnacle Gully over ledged rock for 200 feet then to the top on small holds (300 feet. A. Tewnion; July 1940).

PINNACLE GULLY   300 feet   EASY. GRADE I

First ascent: J. A. Parker and H. Alexander *July 20th 1924*
First winter ascent: Uncertain

A wet scramble in summer. In winter low down there is nothing to distinguish it from the snow slope of the great recess, the features which define it in summer being wiped out by the immense deposit. Near the top it becomes better defined and is heavily corniced.

PINNACLES BUTTRESS   350 feet   DIFFICULT

First ascent: A. Tewnion, S. Tewnion and A. McArthur
September 1941

This is the leftmost of a close-set trio of buttresses forming a detached group on the right of the great recess. It is formed almost entirely of two pinnacles, the higher and smaller of which rises above a narrow col and stands out against the sky even when viewed from a distance.

Above the schrund there is a stretch of scrambling (length depending on time of visit) on low rocks by the side of Pinnacle Gully to the base of an 80-foot crack splitting a slab on the left of the buttress. Climb the crack and go up the balcony of piled boulders above overlooking the gully to a square block covered with vegetation. From the block climb the right wall to a broad ledge and follow this to its end. Here there is a choice of routes to the top of the lower pinnacle. Either traverse to the right across the exposed face then work up on small holds, or surmount a series of mantelshelves on the less exposed north face. From the top of the pinnacle there is a 15-foot descent to the narrow col above which the upper pinnacle rises for 100 feet. There is a choice of several routes but although they are without great difficulty all require care. From the upper pinnacle the plateau is gained by 20 feet of easy rock.

The remaining buttresses of the Pinnacles trio are the steepest rock masses in the corrie. Both are unclimbed as also are the intervening chimneys. Any ascents here would be of a severe nature.

GARBH CHOIRE DHÀIDH

Garbh Choire Dhàidh (pron. "Yay" rhyming with "say") is the right-hand subsidiary of An Garbh Choire. Its cliffs are higher than those of Choire Mòr but it is less savage in aspect. What it lacks in wildness, however, is more than offset by certain features which combine to give it a most cheerful atmosphere. It is open-walled, south-east facing and sun-catching; and from the plateau

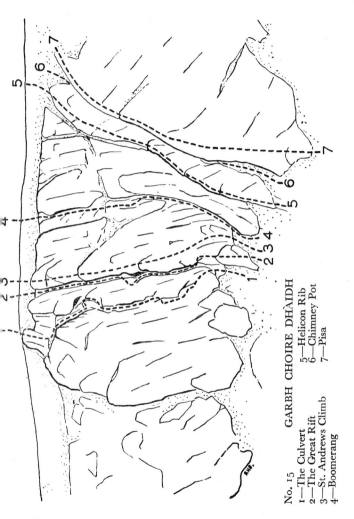

No. 15   GARBH CHOIRE DHÀIDH

1—The Culvert   5—Helicon Rib
2—The Great Rift   6—Chimney Pot
3—St. Andrews Climb   7—Pisa
4—Boomerang

M

rim the young Dee (the finest river source in the country) falls 500 feet to the corrie floor where after running a subterranean course among huge boulders it reappears flowing over a charming turf meadow on which it widens into attractive pools.

The Dee cascade divides the cliff into two parts. To the left the cliff though high and more or less continuous to the entrance of the corrie is vegetated and the rocks lack mass and character. The greatest appeal of this section is in winter. It is then a very steep snow-wall half a mile in length which, tackled at any point, will give grand open-slope work for 800 feet ending in heavy cornices, but as avalanches may occur here and as the run-out in places is over bars of rock care will be necessary.

Two routes are recorded left of the Dee:

MONOLITH GULLY   600 feet MODERATE. GRADE 1

First ascent: W. T. Hendry and G. Lumsden *August 1942*
First winter ascent: M. Scott and G. Sievewright
March 1954

This is the long shallow gully extending the full height of the headland on the left edge of the corrie but hidden from its entrance. It rises to the right of the rock bluffs descending low into the corrie above the pools. It is not a good summer climb.

The bed consists of loose scree with here and there a few wet, slabby pitches. Near the top there is a small cave pitch above which the slabs at the base of the Monolith (which can be seen from the corrie floor) can be climbed direct as can the tooth itself.

Winter: Straightforward 45° snow. Well corniced. Under heavy snow it may be hard to distinguish from the surrounding slopes.

SLAB AND GROOVE   500 feet   DIFFICULT

First ascent: W. T. Hendry and G. Lumsden *August 1942*

Some distance to the left of the Dee cascade two
oblique grooves are seen; the right-hand one is the climb.

Climb the initial 150-foot slab on the right to a small
greasy wall which may be climbed or avoided on the
left after a traverse across the slab. A stretch of feature-
less gully follows with wet and rotten indefinite pitches.
Above this the gully continues as a 150-foot groove to the
plateau. Not a good climb.

DEE WATERFALL   N.C.

First ascent: Dr George Skene Keith and Mr Warren
July 17th 1810

This early scramble was probably made up the right
side of the cascade over grassy slopes and rock outcrops.
The other bank is clothed in vegetation.

The Main Face

The best climbing lies to the right of the cascade on a
grand 450-foot face of granite, part slabby and smooth,
part ribbed and rough. The left side of the face is a
high-angled wall of polished, foliated slabs which angle
into an impressive chimney—the Great Rift; the right
side between the Rift and the Chimney Pot, a deep gully
sunk in an angle formed by a detached buttress on the
extreme right, is divided into ribs and grooves. The
detached buttress whose rocks descend low into the
corrie is Pisa.

From left to right the climbs are:

THE CULVERT   450 feet   SEVERE

First ascent: R. H. Sellers and G. Annand   *July 3rd 1955*

Follows a prominent fault or shelf on the left of the Rift. An exposed climb on grand rock, but an avalanche in 1957 has swept away one of its original features and a little debris may be found on one pitch.

Start 25 feet to left of Rift. Follow slabs for 30 feet to a small platform. Go up the ensuing groove followed by a grassy crack and then climb a wall to a ledge and belay (60 feet). Follow a groove directly over stance for 10 feet then traverse right on to a ledge, thence up a delicate mantelshelf followed by walls to a ledge with avalanche debris (60 feet, piton belay). Climb over flake (part of fall and may not be permanent but wall possibly climbable) to the wall on right then trend slightly left to a waterworn slab (70 feet). Go up the slab on small holds and climb a shallow chimney (100 feet). Above this go up the wall directly under a large overhang and up the slab going left (80 feet). Moderate rock for 40 feet from here to the top.

THE GREAT RIFT   450 feet   VERY DIFFICULT

First ascent: F. R. Malcolm, A. Thom and M. Smith
September 5th 1954

The striking chimney in the centre of the face. One of the best climbs of its kind in the massif. Defined, continuous and affording splendid prospects across and down its surrounding slab-sea. The initial smooth pitch has not been climbed and the chimney is entered some distance above.

Start to the right of the waterslide up a smooth cleanwashed rib then follow a second rib, almost a staircase of holds, to a spindle-shaped rock mass on the right of the chimney (150 feet). Jam and straddle up the inset corner on the right for 35 feet finishing with a strenuous pull-up and enter the Rift below a cave. Leave the cave directly or by the slab on the left and enter another and bigger cave with a great overhanging roof. Climb the slabs on the left then return right and overcome the roof by a short steep wall. (M.S., but recently a piton has been inserted. This may or may not remain in place.) The Rift now opens and is easier. Then comes a slab corner and beyond a bend it narrows once more to a steep, awkward chimney after which several interesting but easier pitches lead to the top.

Winter: A natural ice-trap. Should give one of the best climbs in the massif.

ST. ANDREWS CLIMB   450 feet   SEVERE

First ascent: L. J. Morris and W. S. Yeaman
March 31st 1957

This route is on the fine ridge bounding the right side of Great Rift. The climb at date of writing has not been checked but the line is known to be a good one. It follows a right-angled inset corner running parallel to Great Rift. The original account (in which the heights appear to be exaggerated) is as follows. The start is at the lowest rocks.

1. Up a rib to belay in small cave at foot of main mass (50 feet, D.).
2. Up inset corner until traverse left must be made into large inset corner at 80 feet. This is climbed for 100 feet on grass and rock, then climb wall on right into original groove (100 feet, D.).
3. Go right round corner then climb straight up the wall thence round a corner to stance below small overhang (50 feet, V.D.).

4. Grasp large spike on left and swing round corner to delicate foothold. Traverse left (piton left) back into inset corner. Climb the crack to grass patch and chokestone belay (30 feet, S.).
5. Up inset corner to spike belay under overhanging block (80 feet, D.).
6. Climb to overhang, round it to right then straight up. The final section required three pitons one of which was left (20 feet, S.).
7. Straight up the ridge keeping as near to left edge as possible (100 feet, D.).
8. and 9. Trending slightly right this line followed to top (200 feet, D.).

BOOMERANG   400 feet   VERY DIFFICULT

First ascent: R. H. Sellers and G. Annand

June 12th 1955

A prominent rib coming low down bounds Chimney Pot on its left. This is Helicon Rib. On the left of the open gully which parts Helicon from the main mass is a small arête. Boomerang starts in the groove behind this.

Climb 70 feet to a stance and belay firstly in an easy-angled groove then up a steeper crack. The next pitch is over water-worn rock for 80 feet to a grass ledge. For the ensuing 110 feet the going is moderate but the last 15 feet are more difficult—up a wall with a crack and small chokestone at the top (V.D.). A grass ledge appears. It offers two alternative routes both of which are sporting and good, and an escape downright un-sporting and bad. The escape goes right. Go left, to the foot of a vertical wall nearly 100 feet high which gives a magnificent pitch on good holds (D.) or straight ahead up an 80-foot wall in a recess (V.D.) followed by broken rock to the plateau.

HELICON RIB   450 feet   DIFFICULT

First ascent: K. Winram, R. Porter and J. W. Morgan
April 16th 1949

The prominent rib forming the left wall of the Chimney Pot. The lower section forms a narrow crest of excellent rock with plentiful holds. Above this and beyond a sneck the rock deteriorates and becomes very shattered.

No details required. Follow the defined crest over many good pitches for 250 feet to the sneck. Above this easier ways can be found avoiding difficulty and unpleasantness.

THE CHIMNEY POT 450 feet DIFFICULT. GRADE 2

First ascent: W. T. Hendry and G. Lumsden *August 1942*
First winter ascent: R. H. Sellers and K. A. Grassick
February 1959

This dark chimney-gully should not be mistaken for the Great Rift and vice versa. It is hidden from most viewpoints by the rocks of Pisa.

Climb a 20-foot chimney topped by a chokestone over which water tumbles. Another chokestone pitch of 10 feet follows, after which scree leads to a final gigantic chokestone which has a through route tunnel. Beyond this the sneck on Helicon Rib is reached in 20 feet. Above this the gully is rotten and a way out to the right may be preferred.

Winter: Variable, but steep and usually showing one ice-pitch at the great chokestone, the height of which will depend on the deposit of snow. At the top, the gully forms a wide amphitheatre often heavily corniced.

PISA   500 feet   DIFFICULT

First ascent: J. Tewnion and M. Smith   *August 5th 1951*

The detached, broad-based buttress on the right of the face and forming the right wall of the Chimney Pot. A sporting romp on rough rock, up its left edge.

Low-angled ribs lead to a grass terrace and a prominent overhanging block. Climb the crack on the left of the block to a wall. Go up the wall to a ledge and go left to a mossy recess. Continue up an inset corner to a small ledge on the brink of the Chimney Pot. A short wall ahead leads to further slab and corner pitches trending right to a shattered ledge. Climb into a mossy nook and up the slab on its left. Pleasant scrambling up a piled-block ridge continues to the plateau.

COIRE BHROCHAIN

With thirteen named and unnamed examples Braeriach is pre-eminently the mountain of corries. Of these Coire Bhrochain—on whose cliff edge the summit cairn stands —is perhaps the finest in the Cairngorms proper for cliff-height, scenery and pure corrie form. Remoteness alone has denied it ranking as the playground of the massif, for its cliffs facing south provide pleasurable, non-artificial routes varying greatly in character and generally of medium difficulty. All this on the roughest and cleanest granite. In winter and spring it is unsurpassed for beauty and grandeur.

The cliff is divided by two pronounced breaks into three broad masses, for convenience if not for clarity called West, Central and East Buttresses. On the left is West Buttress separated from Central by West Gully, a broad scree-shoot. Central Buttress is cut off from East

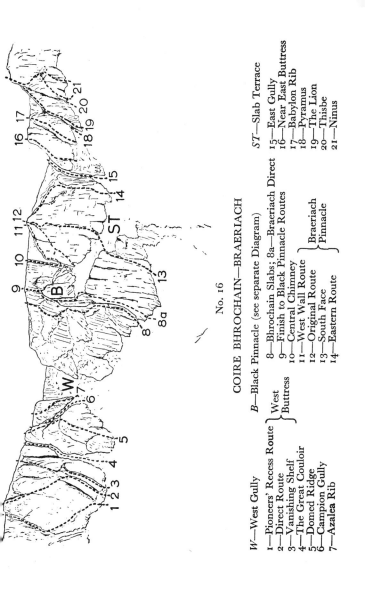

No. 16

COIRE BHROCHAIN—BRAERIACH

W—West Gully

B—Black Pinnacle
ST—Slab Terrace

1—Pioneers' Recess Route
2—Direct Route
3—Vanishing Shelf
4—The Great Couloir
5—Domed Ridge
6—Campion Gully
7—Azalea Rib
} West Buttress

8—Bhrochain Slabs; 8a—Braeriach Direct
9—Finish to Black Pinnacle Routes
10—Central Chimney
11—West Wall Route
12—Original Route
13—South Face
14—Eastern Route
} Braeriach Pinnacle

15—East Gully
16—Near East Buttress
17—Babylon Rib
18—Pyramus
19—The Lion
20—Thisbe
21—Ninus

Buttress by East Gully, narrow for most of its height then funnelling out at the plateau. Each mass is built up of other individual buttresses.

WEST BUTTRESS

The main mass above its easy lower rocks is built up of parallel ribs with intervening slabby corners opening out into funnels of rock of poorer quality—avalanche troughs in winter, water troughs in wet weather. The most striking feature is a great, square summit-tower topping the leftmost rib and to the right of an open chimney. On the right of the main mass and separated from it by the Great Couloir is Domed Ridge which flanks lower West Gully. Branching from West Gully and striking up behind Domed Ridge to the plateau is Campion Gully. Between Campion and upper West Gully is Azalea Rib, a smaller subsidiary of Domed Ridge.

The main mass is less broken than superficial examination suggests and low down the rock is rather smooth. At 700 feet it ranks among the highest continuous cliffs in the Cairngorms.

The climbs left to right are:

PIONEERS' RECESS ROUTE   650 feet   MODERATE

First ascent: A. Harrison and L. St. C. Bartholomew
August 22nd 1925

A flanking route going up the open chimney and recess on the left of the main mass between the square tower and a detached buttress tapering to a spectacular hooked fang. The pioneers gained the chimney after a devious course across the slabs from the lowest point of the buttress but entry can be made directly from below or more easily from the left. (J. 17.200.)

Climb in the chimney or on the right side of it to the recess where short steps lead to the plateau.

DIRECT ROUTE   700 feet   SEVERE

First ascent: A. Stevenson and J. Y. L. Hay
July 17th 1955

Follows the most prominent of the grooves or shelves on the main mass somewhat right of centre, then crosses a dividing rib to finish on the right face of the Tower. A cairn marks the start 100 feet above the screes.

Go up the corner for 150 feet by slabs then a narrow chimney to a spike belay beyond a pointed flake climbed astride. Descend a few feet then climb a steep wall with awkward holds (30 feet) and continue up the groove to a recessed corner (runner) where a left traverse leads on to grass ledges (80 feet, crux). Go up the shallow gully for 100 feet then cross the rib on the left which leads directly to the Tower. Here is magnificent rock. Climb its right flank by a series of steep chimneys.

VANISHING SHELF   650 feet   DIFFICULT. GRADE 3

First ascent: G. H. Leslie and M. Smith   *June 19th 1955*
First winter ascent: R. H. Sellers and K. A. Grassick
February 1959

This is the next prominent shelf to the right of the Direct Route. Its counterpart, but ending at a high balcony overlooking the big pitch in the Great Couloir.

Easy slabs lead to the shelf which is climbed in the corner or on the slabs on the right. Some way up there is a steep wall on the right of a cave. Avoid the wall moving down and right (old piton found here) then go up grooves and reach the balcony by a 15-foot chimney climbed by straddling. The shelf ends here. The wall above is vertical. Go out to the left on a ledge (exposed) and make a long upward traverse to the left. The upper scoop is soon reached and the rock becomes easier. Either climb in the scoop or on the rib on the right to the plateau.

Winter: No details available at time of writing, but the Buttress carries much snow and the line is a good one. Cornices are heavy above this route and are liable to be dangerous.

THE GREAT COULOIR   600 feet   VERY DIFFICULT
GRADE 2–3

First ascent: J. Y. L. Hay   *September 7th 1955*
First winter ascent: J. Y. L. Hay and Miss H. Rose
December 28th 1957

The long, defined gully separating Domed Ridge from the main mass. Above mid-height it bends round a subsidiary rib on the main mass, but straight ahead in the angle between the rib and the left wall is a spectacular 300-foot chimney forming a left branch (Ebony Chimney, unclimbed).

In its lower reaches the couloir is scree-filled, then scrambling over indefinite pitches leads to a long waterslide followed by a chokestone evaded by a line of weakness on the right. A second and bigger chokestone now blocks the couloir. It has not been climbed direct and is passed by taking to the rocks of the Ridge. The piled blocks above this are climbed direct and the final and hardest pitch, a short overhanging groove, is taken by the shelf on the left.

Winter: Named so for its character in winter when it forms a most beautiful chute, very steep in its upper part and heavily corniced, but generally without pitches in mid-season. Before this the summer crux may not be built up and will present a hard ice-pitch (V.S. as on first ascent).

DOMED RIDGE   600 feet   MODERATE. GRADE 3

First ascent: W. D. Brooker and J. W. Morgan
July 26th 1951
First winter ascent: A. G. Mitchell and W. P. L. Thomson
April 9th 1955

Easy pink slabs form a broad base between the Couloir and West Gully. Numerous lines can be taken up the slabs which are seamed by grooves and cracks. Above this the easier way goes right by a series of shelves avoiding a steep tower. Mid-way up, the easy boulder-strewn crest is reached and following this a nick in the ridge leads to the final dome which overhangs directly in front. A low traverse to the right leads to grand climbing up 120 feet of steep, red granite walls and slabs then to the top over easy rock.

Winter: First ascent in rather favourable conditions. The party started on the left and took the tower almost directly by a 60-foot slab and chimney pitch. The Dome provided three pitches on which almost continuous cutting was required. The crux was the last 15 feet of steep rock. Details scant.

CAMPION GULLY   400 feet   DIFFICULT. GRADE 2

First ascent: W. T. Hendry, A. Tewnion and G. Lumsden
August 1942
First winter ascent: K. A. Grassick and A. G. Nicol
April 5th 1954

Between Domed Ridge and Azalea Rib. The left branch of West Gully. Rather grimy in summer.

Above 150 feet of scree comes the first pitch, a 6-foot chokestone. The second 25-foot pitch is steep slab, chokestone and water. More scree leads to the main obstacle, two massive blocks above a cave. A through-route gives access to the second block which is passed on the right. The fourth pitch is also of the cave variety and leads to a final gravel slope.

Winter: One ascent recorded. May have major pitches early in the season but the party were confronted by two small pitches only, although these were found to be rather unsafe owing to drifting powder above ice. A steep double cornice provided an interesting finish. Time: 2½ hours.

AZALEA RIB   300 feet   DIFFICULT

First ascent: K. Winram, C. Petrie and M. Smith
June 28th 1953

The small buttress forming the upper left wall of West Gully. It forms a narrow crest topped by a very steep wall. The crest has not been followed and the existing route goes up the line of least resistance.

Start at the lowest rocks. Go up smooth slabs on the right to a platform then traverse left and make a high step on to the shelf on the right side of the buttress. The shelf, wide at its base, narrows to an awkward moss-grown corner. Beyond this one is virtually off the climb, but double back up a grass gully which leads to a nick on the actual crest above its steep part. Go up slabs on the left to the final vertical wall. Below and to the left is a narrow chokestone chimney. Descend and climb this.

WEST GULLY   500 feet   MODERATE. GRADE I

First ascent: A. Fraser and A. W. Russell

September 10th 1898

First winter ascent: Unknown

The widest break in the cliff, separating West from Central Buttress. It consists of scree and slabs with steeper rocks of no great difficulty at the top.

Winter: Forms a wide and most regular snow corridor, steep at the top and ringed by a big cornice usually entire. A rewarding climb in its unhemmed prospect and surrounding scenery. In good condition, a fast, safe glissade after the cornice is passed.

CENTRAL BUTTRESS

This is a more diversified mass than West. It has several distinctive features. Centrally placed and cut off from the mountain on all sides is the Black Pinnacle— one of the best known features in the Cairngorms. On the left of Black Pinnacle and almost extending to West Gully is a great recessed area of smooth granite—the Bhrochain Slabs. On the right of Black Pinnacle and extending to East Gully is the Braeriach Pinnacle, in reality a big individualistic buttress whose top is almost on a level with the top of the cliffs. Lastly between the foot of Braeriach Pinnacle and the top of the rocks supporting the Black Pinnacle, the Slab Terrace—a natural and easy highway—leads to the heart of the cliff, to the start of the routes on the Black Pinnacle and to Central Buttress Gully. This latter is a broad, hidden shoot striking up the left side of Braeriach Pinnacle.

The climbs left to right are:

BHROCHAIN SLABS   650 feet   VERY DIFFICULT
GRADE 3

First ascent: G. W. Ross and G. O. Clark   *August 1944*
First winter ascent: W. Gault, D. Bruce and A. Milne
February 1960

On the left of Black Pinnacle and from the rocks directly below it a continuous sheer wall drops to Bhrochain Slabs forming a recess. The climb starts at the foot of the recess about 100 feet up and to the left of the lowest rocks of Central Buttress. Good slab climbing on clean, rough rock.

Go up a shallow groove (150 feet) to a platform (cairn) above which is a steep slab split by several cracks. Climb the rightmost of these which starts 30 feet up and slopes to the right. A small platform is reached after 80 feet of difficult climbing. The next objective, a large grass platform up on the left is reached by a hard, smooth slab of easy angle, or by more broken rocks on its right. Above the platform climb another slab using the rightmost of twin cracks set close together to reach yet another platform (at this point a chimney runs down to West Gully and on the right continues up to the saddle behind the Black Pinnacle—see North-West Chimney). From the platform go up the rocks ahead until forced to traverse to the left along an exposed slab, to reach which a short descent is made. A rib on the slab partially blocks the way. Climb this to an excellent pulpit stance. Continue along the slab till it ends then turn a corner and follow a shallow groove with a huge slab on the left to within 50 feet of the plateau where one takes to the rocks on the right and reaches the top of the climb a short distance from the summit cairn.

Winter: No details available at time of writing, but time taken was $4\frac{1}{2}$ hours in perfect conditions with rock-hard snow.

NORTH-WEST CHIMNEY   200 feet   MODERATE

First ascent: G. W. Ross and Miss J. Fleming
September 18th 1948

This strikes up to the saddle of the Black Pinnacle from the Bhrochain Slabs. It originates in an easy fault running up diagonally from the foot of West Gully. The fault crosses Bhrochain Slabs route at the platform above the third pitch. From here the chimney has four choke-stone pitches the last of which is turned by the rough slab on its left.

BRAERIACH DIRECT   750 feet   MILD SEVERE

First ascent: R. H. Sellers, M. Smith and R. W. P. Barclay
September 24th 1956

A direct course from the lowest rocks of the buttress to the plateau which is reached within a short distance east of the mountain's summit. It also provides the best and most direct approach to the routes on the Black Pinnacle. An intriguing route, full of variety and in a splendid environment.

From a frontal view of the buttress the vertical left wall of Black Pinnacle stands out from the cliff like the gnomon of a gigantic sundial—the dial plate being a great 250-foot slab completely isolated by overhangs at its base and sheer walls plunging to Bhrochain Slabs. The object is to gain the Sundial Slab.

Start about 150 feet below the recess of the Slab Route and climb 90 feet of pink, snow-cleaned slab, easy-angled but smooth to a grass terrace. Go up left across the terrace almost to the edge of the recess where two grooves sloping up side by side nestle into the crest on the right. Start in the outer then cross into the higher to reach a belay and cramped stance at the top (V.D.). Cross the

N

crest and traverse upwards to the right on steep, open rock to a stance below a series of cracks and chimneys with little overhangs. Climb these (the upper is V.D.) to a large balcony overlooking the recess and backed by the crest. Progress on this line is barred by overhanging walls. Move down 6 feet and make an awkward crossing over the crest. Traverse along a ledge then back left above to the crest, here a holdless wall of 15 feet. Climb this (S.) then a groove and up over large blocks for 80 feet. Moderate rock leads to a grass terrace below the sharp, vertical edge of the Pinnacle. Here one drops 10 feet to the Sundial Slab.

Climb the Slab close to the Pinnacle wall. The rock is moderate but the Slab ends in space and the first belay comes at the end of the third 90-foot run-out—an insecure position, but full of charm. A 10-foot chimney leads to the platform at the base of the hillward prong of the Pinnacle. After the traverse to the outer prong return and descend to the Pinnacle neck and continue to the plateau by the great smooth slab straight ahead, using a fault leading right.

The Black Pinnacle

The normal approach to the Pinnacle is by the Slab Terrace sloping up left below the rocks of Braeriach Pinnacle. The slab is about 200 feet long and can be walked up and down. It ends in scree below the loose first pitch of Central Buttress Gully which stands between Black Pinnacle on the left and Braeriach Pinnacle on the right. This pitch leads to an amphitheatre where the gully forks. The true gully runs up behind Braeriach Pinnacle; the open left branch to Black Pinnacle neck. The Ordinary Route to the summit is from the neck by this branch. The other routes, Direct and Slab, start below the introductory pitch of the gully.

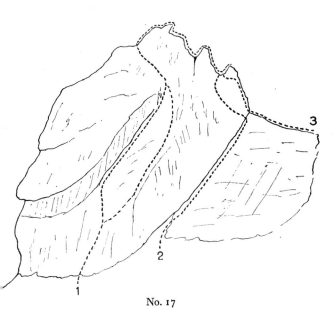

No. 17

BLACK PINNACLE, COIRE BHROCHAIN
Foreshortened view from Slab Terrace

1—Direct Route   2—Slab Route   3—Ordinary Route

ORDINARY ROUTE   500 feet to plateau   MODERATE
GRADE 2

First ascent: J. A. Parker, H. Alexander, J. B. Millar and
W. A. Reid   *October 1911*

Climb the Slab Terrace and the pitch in Central
Buttress Gully and go up to the neck. A short easy
chimney leads to the serrated crest and the outer tooth.

The climb may be continued to the plateau up the
ill-defined rib bordering the great slab on its left on good,
rough rock. This is the more direct line but the pioneers
traversed left from the Pinnacle neck and reached the
plateau by the final easy section of Bhrochain Slabs.

SLAB ROUTE   150 feet   MODERATE

First ascent: W. T. Hendry, A. Tewnion and G. Lumsden
August 1942

This goes up a groove in the slab on the right of the
Pinnacle. At the top the slab overhangs the left branch
of Central Buttress Gully and from this point a traverse
leftwards is made to a point between the hillward prongs.

DIRECT ROUTE   150 feet   DIFFICULT

First ascent: J. H. B. Bell   *June 19th 1938*

At present the best route on the Black Pinnacle.

Approach the Pinnacle directly from the upper end of
the Slab Terrace. Ascent near the left edge appears
impossible because of roof-tile overhangs, but there is a
steep corner at their right edge, roughly in the centre of
the face. Reach this corner by moderate rocks and climb
the narrow crack about 40 feet long set in the angle.
The crack gives access to easier rocks leading back to the
crest on the left and so to the outer prong. (J. 21.434.)

An alternative of similar standard is to climb the exposed right edge overlooking Slab Route by a shallow groove parallel to the 40-foot crack. Steep moderate climbing above leads to the middle prong.

BLACK PINNACLE: WINTER: First winter ascent by the slabs of Slab Route and their snow-ridged outer edge (A. Parker and J. Young, March 1949).

In winter, routes other than the Ordinary from the neck appear too unimportant and artificial to merit grading. The Ordinary Route from the neck and traverse over the prongs under heavy snow is Grade 2. More important is the state of the subsequent snow leading to the summit cornice. Though straightforward it lies mainly on a foundation of slab and is prone to avalanche.

CENTRAL BUTTRESS GULLY   500 feet from base at Slab Terrace   MODERATE. GRADE 1

First ascent (winter): W. N. Ling and H. Raeburn
April 20th 1908

Apart from the slab at the start and the pitch (40 feet) leading to the amphitheatre all is easy. The main gully which bounds the left side of Braeriach Pinnacle leads to the plateau and is chiefly scree.

From the amphitheatre Central Chimney provides the better climb and natural continuation in summer.

Winter: A long interesting climb from the corrie floor wending a way through grand scenery and often heavily corniced. No pitches, but exposed to the risk of avalanches whose natural outfall is over the high rocks below the Slab Terrace.

CENTRAL CHIMNEY   300 feet   MODERATE

First ascent: W. T. Hendry, A. Tewnion and G. Lumsden
August 1942

This is the narrow chimney cleaving the wall of the amphitheatre to the plateau in a direct line with the pitch of Central Buttress Gully.

Wet in its lower reaches it improves with height. There are three chimney pitches, the first about 100 feet up topped by a chokestone. The first and second may be taken directly or by-passed on the left on steep, rough rock.

Braeriach Pinnacle

The biggest feature of Central Buttress, lying between Central Buttress Gully and East Gully and above the Slab Terrace.

Its time-honoured name is rather misleading, for only from the plateau does it show any trace of pinnacle form. In reality it is a broad-based buttress whose rocks sloping up from right to left end on their steep left edge in a ridge formed by an undercut wall overhanging upper Central Buttress Gully.

Variations can and have been made at random on the frontal face and all have tended to be of similar character. Only the older established routes are therefore noted: Original on the left, South Face in the centre and Eastern on the right. The finest course on the Pinnacle and one of the best on the mountain, is West Wall Route which goes up the edge or ridge overlooking Central Buttress Gully.

WEST WALL ROUTE   300 feet   MILD SEVERE

First ascent: A. Tewnion, W. T. Hendry and G. Lumsden
August 1942

Excellent rock, steep and exposed.

Start just above the pitch in Central Buttress Gully and traverse to the right to a small platform on the edge of the Pinnacle. Climb on the right of the edge by steep and difficult rock to gain a second platform, smaller and 50 feet above the first (piton belay). Continue directly up the arête or the steep wall just to the right (60 feet). Follow a quartz vein straight up the exposed edge overlooking the Gully until it is possible to traverse right into a groove which leads back to the crest at a broad platform. The angle now eases and it is a pleasant scramble along an airy ridge to the top of the Pinnacle.

ORIGINAL ROUTE   400 feet   DIFFICULT

First ascent: P. D. Baird and R. N. Traquair
March 27th 1931

Several routes have been described on or near this line of ascent and much variation is possible over sound rock with strips of vegetation.

Start below the pitch in Central Buttress Gully and ascend to the right on good slabs until the line of a shallow gully leads to the summit crest.

SOUTH FACE   700 feet   DIFFICULT

First ascent: J. Sutherland and P. D. Ritchie
June 22nd 1931

Start just to right of the lowest rocks of Central Buttress below the Slab Terrace and climb by ribs and grooves of good rock to reach the Terrace at its narrowest point. Cross the Terrace here and climb more or less directly to the summit on the right of a recess on very rough granite allowing a choice of route.

The original party went right and then straight up, keeping East Gully just in sight. About 100 feet from the top a traverse was made to the left and then up piled blocks to the summit.

EASTERN ROUTE   500 feet   MODERATE

First ascent: C. G. Cowie, S. R. Tough and G. L. Ritchie
July 1933

Follow the edge of East Gully for about 350 feet then go obliquely up to the summit over broken rock.

BETWEEN Braeriach Pinnacle and East Buttress is the deep-set East Gully:

EAST GULLY   500 feet   MODERATE. GRADE 1

First ascent (winter): J. Drummond, T. Gibson and A. W. Russell   *April 5th 1901*
First summer ascent: W. T. Hendry, L. Durno, G. Morrison and W. L. Walker   *July 1940*

In summer this gully is wet and harbours a series of steps rising out of a bed of scree. Little difficulty is found in passing these. It is usually snow-filled far into the summer.

Winter: A straight-cut chute, narrow with no pitches. The wide upper funnel is usually well corniced but with an easy exit on the right. Given the right conditions, an exhilarating glissade can be had to the corrie floor.

East Buttress

Unlike West and Central this is composed of smaller,

more individualistic buttresses set side by side and divided by deep chimneys or gullies. Bordering East Gully is Near East Buttress, separated from Babylon Rib on its right by a short, narrow chimney. On the right of Babylon is Pyramus, a gully with a pointed dividing rib low down giving it a double-barrelled start. An attractive ridge, the Lion, separates Pyramus from his Thisbe—a deep, twisting gully. Finally on the extreme right stands Ninus, steepest and largest of the buttresses.

The rock is everywhere the roughest, but frost action and lack of traffic dictate a cautious use of some of the more choice-looking holds.

The climbs left to right:

NEAR EAST BUTTRESS   300 feet   MODERATE

First ascent: I. M. Brooker, A. Lyall and D. McConnach
March 27th 1948

Start on the edge of East Gully and scramble up, firstly over rock then grass up to the right to the base of the buttress well to the right of the gully. Go straight ahead up the left edge of the steep portion of the buttress. Moderate climbing with many good, varied pitches on fine, rough rock to the top.

Much harder routes can be found on the right overlooking the chimney between the buttress and Babylon Rib.

The left edge overlooking East Gully is a scramble, bottom to top.

BABYLON RIB   300 feet   MODERATE

First ascent: G. C. Greig, M. Smith and K. Winram
March 1st 1953

In two parts; a narrow, wedge-shaped lower section

and above a large platform, a narrow ridge to the plateau. Entertaining.

Steep but moderate rock leads up for 60 feet to an open corner above a ledge. Climb the corner and in 30 feet comes a slab with a thin crack. Above this move left to the chimney then cross the rib and climb a groove overlooking Pyramus to a platform. From here to the top the climbing is up an amusing arête of rounded granite.

PYRAMUS   350 feet   MODERATE. GRADE 1

First ascent. W. T. Hendry and G. Lumsden *August 1942*
First winter ascent: W. D. Brooker and S. McPherson
April 12th 1950

Low down, the rock in the gully is sound and waterworn; higher up it degenerates into gravel. A pointed rib at the foot furnishes the gully with two branches. These join about 200 feet up. Climb in the right branch (the left is unpleasant).

Start from a shallow basin and climb to the junction over pitches of good clean rock and waterworn slab. (The dividing rib is a good alternative.) Beyond this the climbing lies up easy slabs until the rock degenerates. The gully forks about 80 feet from the top. The right fork provides a poor finish; the left is better—a chimney with a final chokestone of rough rock.

Winter: Under conditions of heavy snow there are no pitches but in a mild season rock may begin to show in March. It might then sport glazed slab pitches owing to alternate thaw and freeze. It may be heavily corniced but is not usually so. Early in the season the start by the left branch (which is narrow) is the more sporting.

THE LION   370 feet   DIFFICULT

First ascent: K. Winram, R. Porter and J. W. Morgan
April 17th 1949

A rather attractive ridge with steep walls falling into Thisbe on the right.

The start is up very steep rock on the left of the crest. Holds are plentiful but lower down use these with caution. The crest is gained, after many interesting moves, in about 100 feet. Climb the crest, which lands one at a small pinnacle. After a level promenade keep going up to the right on the rocks overlooking Thisbe. These maintain their interest to the plateau.

THISBE   370 feet   DIFFICULT. GRADE 3

First ascent: W. T. Hendry and G. Lumsden *August 1942*
First winter ascent: G. H. Leslie and M. Smith
January 3rd 1955

Though short, the best gully climb in the corrie summer or winter. It is well-defined by high walls and the rock is clean and waterworn.

Climb over blocks, slabs, and up a smooth sloping wall leading to a bend. Beyond this there are more slab pitches with intervening chokestones up to a point where the gully narrows to a steep, thin crack. Climb the crack directly or ascend the right wall. Above this comes the final pitch—a large chokestone climbed on the left. Scree to the plateau.

Winter: The most promising conditions will be found in the first and second months of the year. Later than this some of the good things may be banked out, but all depends on snowfall.

On the first ascent it presented four ice-pitches. The first was in the groove leading to the sloping wall; and on the wall itself an ice-runnel went up the angle to the bend and continued round this to a chokestone overcome by straddling. Steep snow then led to a high pitch with an overhanging boss of ice surmounted with the aid of an ice-piton and sling. The last impressive pitch was turned by a steep traverse on to the rocks on the right and the gully regained by a ledge. Exit was on the left flank. Time: $3\frac{3}{4}$ hours.

NINUS	400 feet	DIFFICULT

First ascent: (*a*) G. C. Greig and J. Tewnion
           (*b*) K. Winram, G. Dey and M. Smith
           June 29th 1952

Ninus is the steep buttress on the extreme right of the corrie forming the right wall of Thisbe. It is marked at mid-height by a great rock scar. Two routes, meeting at less than mid-height, have been made.

(*a*) Start on a prominent rib low to the right of the buttress. This gives pleasant scrambling to an inset corner pitch formed by a slab and a large block. A similar pitch follows then a depression is entered. Here the routes meet.

(*b*) Start on the extreme left in line with the first pitch of Thisbe. From a white ledge climb a very steep wall then up a groove followed by a steep nose. A good belay is found at 90 feet where the angle eases. Ten feet higher go up an awkward step to the right and make a long traverse across the glacis below the overhanging centre section of the buttress. At the end of the traverse an upward movement round a nose leads to the depression of (*a*) and the routes meet.

Immediately above on the left a steep chimney-groove is started on the right and finished on the left over rock split and broken by the great rock-fall. Easier climbing leads to the scar. Another chimney-groove leads out to the crest on the left and ends at a small, undercut platform on the brink of Thisbe. The pitch above is a delightful, airy rib of 60 feet on the edge of Thisbe, on vertical rough rock with good holds. A final short pitch leads to easy ground.

THE CLIMBS ON THE DEVIL'S POINT, BEINN BHROTAIN AND CÀRN A' MHAIM

THESE are fine, rough, interesting mountains differing widely in character but consistent in their rocks being indefinite, or short, or vegetated. They have redeeming values to the climber, however. Two provide good winter climbing and all three short and difficult problems within easy reach of a comfortable base. This is Corrour Bothy at the foot of The Devil's Point.

THE DEVIL'S POINT

This striking headland which contributes in no small measure to the great character of the Lairig Ghru is in spite of its fierce appearance most disappointing to the climber. Much apparently attractive ground is in fact unstable vegetation and loose rock. The whole face may be wandered over save at the northerly belt of slabs topped by its overhangs. Here many hard, short climbs have been made, but the unvarying nature of the terrain makes them all rather stereotyped and unimportant.

Only the well-established routes (which go up the more natural lines) have been mentioned. All involve about 1000 feet of scrambling.

In winter the mountain improves greatly and the three gullies and more easy lines give long Grade 1 climbs. The Dee face assumes an Alpine aspect and can, after heavy snow, give fine climbing involving route-finding, ice, and much step-cutting. A recommended line goes up the open chimney below the south end of the overhangs and continues past the overhangs to the steep slopes and ribs above. The Geusachan face after heavy snow is often the scene of great avalanches, but these generally occur off the climbing routes.

CORROUR SLABS
DIFFICULT

First ascent: Dr Hobson, W. L. Walker and W. T. Hendry
March 1940

This starts behind the bothy and goes up the steep, smooth slabs to the right of the main line of overhangs by a system of grass cracks. The overhang is passed at its lowest point by a short, difficult chimney. (Harder lines can be followed.) Easy scrambling leads to a wide, shallow gully, which is a walk.

AT the south end of the Dee face an open depression strikes up to the summit. This is South-East Gully—slabby and loose. Between this and South-West Gully just inside Glen Geusachan is the South-East Corner—a scramble (S. H. Cowan and E. B. Robertson, April 1908). South-West Gully lies above a great white scree-runnel and is easy. The steeper rocks on its left edge are South-West Arête.

SOUTH-WEST ARÊTE
DIFFICULT

First ascent: A. Parker and J. Young
March 1949

Follow the scree of S.W. Gully to a rock and heather step. Climb this on the right for 80 feet then traverse left to the Arête reached at an ill-defined sentry box. A difficult corner leads to the crest of the rib which is followed to a little tower. Above, broken rock leads to vegetation. Artificial.

GEUSACHAN GULLY 800 feet MODERATE. GRADE I

First ascent: An unknown party in 1926

This is the large gully well to the left of South-West. It is more defined than the others and cuts back diagonally to the summit. A good climb in winter; defined and steep.

Prominent steep slabs lead up to the bed which continues slabby to an amphitheatre at the top where several ways out can be found.

THE mountain continues westward into Glen Geusachan as a great wall of slab. The only feature hereabouts is the Devil's Cave, perched in the midst of the slabs, two thirds up the face in a steep wall facing up the glen. It is hidden from the Dee approach and is reached by turf ledges from the west. The first visit recorded was in 1929. Since then visits have been rare, but (for the record) it has been used as sleeping quarters by seekers after the unusual on more than one occasion.

BEINN BHROTAIN

The Dee Face: Towards the river the mountain presents a face of small indefinite ribs and buttresses flanked by glaciated slabs. Hard steep climbing may be found, but artificial and of no great length (200 feet). The most important features are the slabs on the left; a hanging recess in the centre with steep rocks on its left; and on the right a defined gully short of the scree-shoot facing up river.

GREEN GULLY   300 feet   MODERATE

The defined gully. An easy climb summer and winter offering a direct route to the summit of the mountain from Derry Lodge.

The first pitches, one indefinite, the other a chokestone with a through route, are easy, but near the top there is moderate climbing over a chokestone above a narrower section (M. Smith and C. Petrie, September 1949).

The gully is steep and straightforward under snow (B. Furmiston and D. Hilton; J. Kershaw and G. Whitham, April 1952).

Coire Cath nam Fionn: This corrie forming the northwest face of Beinn Bhrotain is one of the most secluded spots in the Cairngorms. Here high on the left at the entrance is the best piece of rock on the mountain—Fingal's Buttress on which there is one route. The rest of the face to the Bhrotain–Monadh Mor col is composed of vegetated buttresses with two defined gullies giving good Grade 1 climbs.

TIERED CRACKS   300 feet   VERY DIFFICULT

First ascent: K. Winram, G. C. Greig and M. Smith
June 8th 1952

Fingal's Buttress is composed of very steep slabby rock on its left and centre; on its right it throws down ribs into a scree-filled amphitheatre. From the corrie floor a crack can be seen rising in three short sections up the edge where the slabs and ribs meet. This is the climb.

Broken rocks lead to a level grass platform. A small slab and a groove trending left lead to a little wall and another platform. Climb the first tier of the crack lying hard in the corner. Avoid the steep second tier by going out on a ledge to the right. From a scooped slab move up round a projecting nose to a little glacis. A cat-crawl to the left leads to the third tier. Climb the crack and continue straight up the wall to the sharp edge above. From a niche on the arête climb a steep nose above to

o

easy ground. The slabs straight ahead in line with the buttress edge may be followed to a difficult chimney overlooking the amphitheatre.

THE GULLIES "A" (300 FEET) AND "B" (450 FEET)

No winter ascent of "A" (the leftmost gully) has been recorded. It should give a sporting climb, the steeper and better of the two. "B" is straightforward (first winter ascent: P. D. Baird and R. N. Traquair, March 29th 1931).

Both gullies have been climbed in summer (C. Petrie and M. Smith, September 1950). "A" is more defined and is entered over slabs. There is a pitch in the right branch immediately above a fork, thereafter only short steps. "B" after a short scramble at the start is mainly scree.

CÀRN A' MHAIM

The mountain on its Dee face offers diversions fit for an evening's entertainment from Corrour Bothy. High up opposite the bothy there are short steep problems on ribs and slabs (80–90 feet) and further north near the Allt Clach nan Taillear is the Palette, a curious, inclined slab aptly named from its shape and colour. The ascent of this from its widest point going directly up to and over the most prominent overhanging corner at the top is a good "night-cap". The lower slabs, although moderately inclined, are smooth and give two very hard moves (one moving out from an overhanging right-angled corner, the other at a holdless step at mid-height). The overhung corner at the top is a good severe using a piton and a shoulder. The easiest line breaks out right some 80 feet below the corner. (250 feet in length. J. Gadd and Mrs Gadd, July 1955.)

On the east side of the mountain the sections of slab overlooking Glen Luibeg are of little interest other than making for sporting lines to the summit from Derry Lodge. Various routes have been made ranging up to V.D. The earliest records date from 1940. The best route to the summit in winter from this direction lies up the little tapering gully in the recess between the slabs.

THE BUTTRESSES OF SGÒRAN DUBH MÒR AND SGÒR GAOITH

LOCH EINICH (1650 feet) set in its great U shaped trough between Braeriach and Sgòr Gaoith is surpassed only by Loch Avon in the Cairngorms for savage grandeur. This it owes to five great buttresses thrown down to within 600 feet of its western shore by the summits of Sgòran Dubh Mòr (3635 feet) and Sgòr Gaoith (3658 feet)—1400 feet of complicated, discontinuous ribs and arêtes, slabs and pillars, extending along their straight base-line for a distance of nearly two miles.

Access being comparatively easy from a centre on a railway main line, this climbing ground was the first to be opened up by the pioneers in the Cairngorms proper. Their climbs hallowed by the years were comparatively well known and for long other and better climbing areas in the Cairngorms suffered neglect by later parties.

As is often the case with early exploration, many routes of the pioneers are difficult to trace, and even now thorough investigation has not altogether clarified the scene.

Although climbers will find that two only of the five buttresses give climbing of the first class, the cliffs above Loch Einich are amongst the finest features of the Cairngorms, intriguing in their complexity and ideally suited to random exploration.

APPROACHES

From Aviemore to Colyumbridge by public road thence by rough road to the site of the Upper Bothy in Glen Einich. There is a locked gate just beyond Achnagoichan and cars are not allowed beyond this point. The

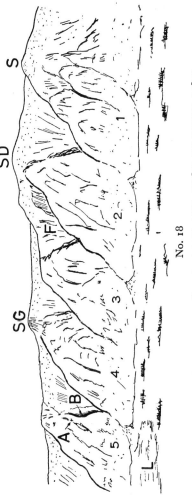

No. 18

BUTTRESSES OF SGÒR GAOITH AND SGÒRAN DUBH MÒR

SG—Sgòr Gaoith
L—Loch Einich
F—Fan Corrie

SD—Sgòran Dubh Mòr
A—A' Chailleach
1, 2, 3, 4 & 5—Buttresses

S—Sgòran Dubh Beag
B—No. 5 Buttress Gully

best means of access is by bicycle (hirer in Aviemore)
and these can be ridden to Loch Einich. Distance from
Aviemore: 9 miles.

N.B.   (*a*) No camping is allowed in Glen Einich.
        (*b*) The Upper and Lower Bothies of the 1″ map
               are no longer in existence.
        (*c*) The outflow from the loch is strong and there
               are few crossing places. Cross at the old
               sluice by stepping-stones.

THE BUTTRESSES

The two miles long face as seen from the Einich road
is divided into six defined buttresses but the first and
second of these have in the traditional nomenclature been
treated as one. To avoid confusion this method has been
retained and the buttresses numbered 1–5 from north to
south i.e. right to left.

An apt description of the crags is found in an early
article in the S.M.C.J.:

It is as though four gigantic funnels or wine-fillers had been
let into the rock, the splayed-out portion being a high upper
corrie often fringed with rock and the stroup a very steep
water-slide. The five rock-masses thus separated take much
the same form reversed, a broad and steep buttress narrowing
towards the top and breaking away into a spectacular ridge
of low angle and no difficulty. Each mass is cut by gullies and
chimneys into several arêtes, more or less continuous.

Many of the courses were worked out at an Easter
Meet of the S.M.C. in 1902, but snow masking the lower
rocks, gullies and ledges at that time coupled with the
rather vague accounts of the pioneers has led to some
confusion and at least three of their climbs are hard to
locate precisely. Since then finer routes have been made,
especially on 1 and 2 Buttresses which offer the most
continuous rock-climbing on the face.

The climbs on 1 and 2 Buttresses are mainly in the region of 400 feet but scrambling on the spectacular but easy upper ridges adds greatly to the total height. It is indeed often awkward to traverse off a climb and it is usually necessary to follow these upper ridges almost to their end. Buttresses 3, 4 and 5 are more vegetated and ledged, but have fine individual features—short, steep walls, deep chimneys, towers and pinnacles.

The rock is generally sound and rough and vegetation where present is chiefly heather.

For climbers whose acquaintance with the crags is limited three climbs are specially recommended: Roberts' Ridge, Rose Ridge and Diamond Buttress.

The buttresses being numbered from right to left the individual climbs are treated in like manner and described as one sees them when passing along the loch to the head of the glen.

No. 1 BUTTRESS

As already indicated this mass is composed of two buttresses separated by the first outstanding gully on the face—the Willow Spout or Sput Seilich. These buttresses are henceforth described as the Northern and Southern Sections of No. 1 Buttress.

THE NORTHERN SECTION

This, the rightmost, presents a slabby face to the glen. Its finest feature is a grand steep-nosed buttress bordering the Willow Spout. On the right the buttress falls into a gully with a long white scree-shoot. Immediately to the right of the gully are two distinct ribs. The right hand one is the first climb on the face.

PINNACLE RIB   350 feet   DIFFICULT

First ascent: G. S. Ritchie and J. G. Ferguson
May 15th 1948

Separated from the left hand rib by a little gully. One third up, the rib is crossed by a broad ledge attainable by various ways.

Start at a cairn below the left end of the ledge and climb a difficult 40-foot buttress then move a little right along the ledge to a chimney. Climb the chimney to a narrower ledge. The pinnacle above may be avoided by a wall on the right, but the route goes left to a groove behind the pinnacle. Continue up beyond the pinnacle to reach easy ground.

No. 1 BUTTRESS RIB   250 feet   VERY DIFFICULT

First ascent: J. B. Hyne, F. L. Swinton and R. Harper
October 5th 1953

The small rib between Pinnacle Rib and the main mass of the Northern Section. In two sections; a broad steep lower part then a narrow upper ridge.

Head up grassy ledges to a rowan tree (50 feet) then go left and climb a corner with bad rock. From the top of a block move right on to a slab, delicate in its upper part. At the top follow the narrow horizontal arête ahead to the foot of the upper section. Follow the defined ridge.

THE main mass of the Northern Section is a fine clean-cut buttress springing from the screes between the Willow Spout and the gully with the white scree-shoot. The steep and defined nose on the brink of Willow Spout is

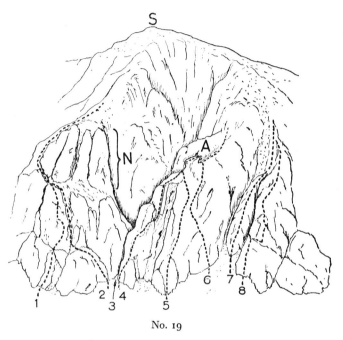

No. 19

SGÒRAN DUBH—No. 1 BUTTRESS

S—Sgòran Dubh Beag   *N*—Northern Rampart   *A*—The Anvil

1—Central Route   4—Roberts' Ridge   7—No. 1 Buttress Rib
2—Original Route   5—Cram's Route   8—Pinnacle Rib
3—The Willow Spout   6—Crowberry Rib and Slabs

Roberts' Ridge which rises for 450 feet and terminates in a knife-edge above a curious granite structure called The Anvil. To the right of the Ridge the buttress is cleft by the turfy Central Chimney, beyond which two routes go up to join the Ridge in its upper part. That on the right is Crowberry Rib and Slabs, starting well up the white shoot and ending at the knife-edge above The Anvil. That on the left is Cram's Route, which goes up the right side of Central Chimney to meet the Ridge below The Anvil. (N.B. This is Cram's Route "B" of the C.G. 1950. Cram's Route "A" of that guide follows an indirect course from a point left of Central Chimney to the upper steep section of the Ridge, missing out the good things on that route. It is herein treated as a variant to the Ridge.)

CROWBERRY RIB AND SLABS 400 feet DIFFICULT

First ascent: J. H. B. Bell and Mrs Bell *October 10th 1947*

With the exception of its final pitch the upper section of this climb is vegetated and often unpleasant.

Move right from Roberts' Ridge past Central Chimney to a well-broken ridge on the left of the white scree-shoot. Go up the ill-defined rib in three pitches of 60 feet, 15 feet and 60 feet respectively to a heather platform then follow heather for 50 feet to a little chimney ending in a blaeberry ledge. Move left round a corner and ascend directly for 40 feet, thence by another 40 feet of heather-clad rock gain the Crowberry Orchard. The next pitch inclines right by slabs and cracks for 60 feet. Further heather leads to a long, rather difficult section of grooves and slabs finishing at the knife-edge on Roberts' Ridge.

CRAM'S ROUTE   450 feet   VERY DIFFICULT

First ascent: A. L. Cram and Miss E. C. Bailey

July 21st 1935

This is Cram's Route "B" of the C.G. 1950. The original start was at the foot of Central Chimney up the right-hand ridge (J. 20.459) but the better way is to round the ridge to its foot and start directly upwards.

There is little difficulty for some way until a vertical slab compels a traverse to the right. Climb the first vertical inset corner (V.D.), then by bearing left it becomes easier to a scramble up a grass gully on the right to the foot of a chimney with a projecting constriction. Above the through-route so formed fine climbing up airy slabs with grand holds leads to Roberts' Ridge below the Anvil.

ROBERTS' RIDGE   450 feet   MILD SEVERE

First ascent: J. H. B. Bell, E. E. Roberts and D. W. Howe

April 24th 1938

Named in honour of a 64th birthday. The climb is now deservedly popular—the best to date in Glen Einich. The finish which is totally unexpected adds to its character. Excellent rock. Recommended.

Start close to the Willow Spout and climb steep but moderate rock for 50 feet to the foot of a tree growing in the base of a narrow chimney. Use the tree firstly to reach a niche above, then as a belay. Go up a short chimney (D.) to a belay then move up and slightly right, returning higher to the left—steep and exposed; finally by a bad step up to the right where there is a smooth slab. Belay above. Easier climbing straight ahead ends the lower steep section.

The intermediate section is straight ahead: moderate

but interesting rock with plenty of stances ending at the upper steep wall of 60 feet which is almost severe.

Ascend a long fissure, not deep but nearly vertical in places; an awkward bit at mid-height but good holds near the top. There is a good wedging stance above. (It is possible to avoid this fissure on the left but it should not be missed.) Above this is another short, steep section then easy scrambling to a crack on the left side giving access to the slabby roof of the Anvil. Now there is an awkward gap—difficult for the last man as there is exposure on either side. It is an 8-foot drop to a knife-edge. From here the ridge broadens to the plateau. (J. 7.82, 22.135.)

Variation: Start at the foot of Central Chimney up the wall on the left by vegetated ledges veering left to gain Roberts' Ridge at the upper steep 60-foot wall below the Anvil. (Difficult. A. L. Cram, no date. J. 20.459.)

THE WILLOW SPOUT 500 feet to the forks GRADE 1

First ascent (*winter*): G. T. Glover, —. Leathart and R. W. Worsdell   *March 28th 1902*
First summer ascent: A. L. Cram (J. 19.142)

The most defined gully on the face but suited for winter climbing only. It is contained by high rock walls and is divided in its upper part by a big rock buttress—unclimbed, but unattractive. The main gully contains one pitch—60 feet of slab 200 feet from the mouth. The right branch is uninteresting; the left branch has a few short pitches but is wet and unpleasant. The gully is not a good means of descent in summer.

Winter: A long Grade 1 climb by the right branch. The left branch is more sporting, steeper and more direct—900 feet to the summit ridge. Scenery repaying.

Good for a long safe glissade at peak in the right branch.
(J. 7.82; C.C.J. 10.228.)

THE SOUTHERN SECTION

The main feature of this section of No. 1 Buttress is a
fine wall at about one third of its height. This wall
completely blocks the way from the steep crags of the
lower buttress to the easy converging ridges leading to
the rise on the summit ridge of Sgòran Dubh Mòr. (This
rise or point is often erroneously called Sgòran Dubh
Beag, the local name for Sgòr Gaoith.) The wall is the
Northern Rampart, 150 feet high and almost vertical,
forming a smooth, forbidding band of rock girdling the
buttress—granite in its least co-operative mood.

There is no connection between the routes on the
Rampart and routes leading to it from below where
much variation is possible.

Routes below the Rampart

ORIGINAL ROUTE   400 feet   MODERATE

First ascent: H. Kynaston, W. A. Mounsey and H. Rae-
    burn   *March 30th 1902*

An indefinite summer route, mainly scrambling. On
the first ascent the rocks were covered with fresh snow.

Easy scrambling from the foot of Willow Spout up the
buttress for 100 feet. At this point make a considerable
left traverse to turn a steep slabby face on the south by an
open chimney harbouring a rowan tree (close here to
Central Route). Above this a long subsidiary arête runs
up to the left to abut against the southern end of the
Rampart, but it is easier to scramble up the correspond-
ing gully on the right (J. 7.82, 122, 274).

CENTRAL ROUTE   350 feet   VERY DIFFICULT

First ascent: G. S. Ritchie and H. I. Ogilvy   *April 7th 1940*

Goes up the north edge of a distinct, tapering wall to join the arête on the Original Route. The wall lies above and to the right of a prominent, forked tongue of scree.

A moderate 70-foot rib leads to a grassy scoop. Walk left to an arête formed by the edge of the central wall. Climb 70 feet up the edge to a small stance then along ledge to the left and up an exposed chimney. Step left round on to the face and climb a crack with small, jammed stones to a ledge. Step left on to the face again and climb another chimney and join the shattered subsidiary arête leading to the south end of the Rampart. (J. 23.43.)

Two other routes are recorded below the Rampart, but details are scant and for one route non-existent. These climbs have not been traced. The details are thus:

OGILVY'S ROUTE: "220 feet of very difficult climbing on clean rock, then 70 feet severe slab for which rubbers are advised." This route is probably on the very steep wall to the left of Central Route. (H. I. Ogilvy and Miss L. S. Robson, August 1940 (*Cambridge Mountaineering* 1940).

CRAM'S ROUTE: "on the southern portion of the crag" (J. 19.283).

Routes on the Northern Rampart

This imposing bastion is built of four extremely steep, slabby buttresses with intervening recesses. It is some 150 feet in height—not perhaps high enough to warrant its notoriety. Face-climbing is problematical—the granite although rough offers few holds and these are rounded. Details of routes are again fragmentary and the exact location of climbs is open to conjecture.

(a) The normal way of overcoming the Rampart after ascending Central or Original Routes is to traverse left from the top of the subsidiary arête and climb a slabby chimney of no great difficulty (Moderate).

(b) The first ascent of the Rampart proper was made by A. L. Cram and C. E. Maconochie in May 1931. They climbed the southern portion direct from the end of the subsidiary arête by an "unmistakable cleft, overcome by the rough texture of the rock" (J. 19.283).

(c) Ogilvy's Route cannot unfortunately be traced owing to lack of detail. "Two pitches, 50 and 90 feet respectively, up the main wall. Then two very difficult pitches to the top" (Very severe in rubbers. H. I. Ogilvy and Miss L. Scott Robson, August 18th 1940).

(d) There is a record of N. E. Odell at Easter 1934 climbing the wall at its northern end: "60 feet of slabs to a ledge; a further 50 feet of slabs gave access to a larger ledge. Thereafter easy ground to a snow gully finish on the north side of the buttress. The slabs were exposed and the holds poor."

From the easy gully of the Original Route (q.v.) it is comparatively straightforward to traverse right below the mass of the Rampart to gain a small airy platform below the forbidding slabby nose of its northern part. No further rightward traverse towards the left branch of the Willow Spout is possible and the rock above is most uncompromising. It seems therefore that Odell traversed into the gully below this point after ascending the right edge of the buttress and was not actually on the Rampart proper.

(e) During investigation for this guide an attempt was made on the first depression to the left of the slabby nose of this north section of the Rampart. This was repulsed at the second of two overhangs which crown the depression. Up to that point the rock was treacherous. Accidents have happened here and this line is not recommended to future parties.

Above the Rampart

Continuing up the moderate chimney by-passing the Rampart on the left, no further difficulties are met with although the crag narrows and several towers are overcome on the way to the summit ridge.

No. 2 BUTTRESS

This and No. 3 Buttress constitute the largest mass of rock on the face. They are separated by the deep Fan Corrie at the head of which stands the peak of Sgòran Dubh Mòr. Fan Corrie drains into the narrow 2/3 Gully lower down. The buttress consists of a number of quite distinct ridges which converge near a grassy col high up. The intervening gullies contain mixed rock and grass and offer sport under snow only.

The key to the rock-mass adjoining 2/3 Gully is Bachelors' Chimney. The remaining ridges are not complicated.

The early records of climbs on this buttress lack precision. The following accounts have been compiled after careful checking though even now, after prolonged investigation, the exact lines of two routes are not established.

From right to left the rocks gain height in marked progression. From the site of the Upper Bothy a prominent Y-shaped scree-shoot can be seen lying almost mid-way between the lowest rocks on the right and 2/3 Gully on the left. The angle of the Y is formed by the wedge of Decoy Ridge which is separated on its right by a deep recess from another narrow, steep ridge bending sharply above the recess to join Decoy Ridge about 250 feet up. This is the Minaret, the first climb from the right.

THE MINARET   250 feet   DIFFICULT

First ascent: T. W. Patey and D. Scott.   *August 30th 1954*

A short, sporting route on good rock. Go up a steep arête for 150 feet. The arête culminates in a deep crack to the top of a tower. After another short pitch scrambling leftwards leads to Decoy Ridge.

DECOY RIDGE   450 feet   DIFFICULT

First ascent: Unknown

The name is prompted by the fact that this has been climbed many times by parties under the impression that it was Rose Ridge, as which climb it was previously, but erroneously, described.

Indefinite scrambling up the buttress leads naturally to the right of a square, sleek slab below a prominent step. Traverse left below an overhang above the slab to an open corner which may be climbed in several ways. From here easy climbing offering much variation leads to the top.

ROSE RIDGE   500 feet to grass col   VERY DIFFICULT

First ascent: W. A. Morrison, W. C. Newbigging and
    A. E. Robertson   *April 29th 1904*

One of the best climbs on the face. The climbing is well defined and interesting throughout with many good pitches, narrow and of a difficult standard.

The ridge lies left of Decoy Ridge directly above a

P

long, thin, sandy runnel. It is marked by the conspicuous rock-wall which forms the north flank high up, and by trees growing out of it a little lower on the same side.

Start up a rib of low angle. In a short distance the rib narrows to an easy arête with one or two little, steep pitches. At one point slightly higher, daylight may be seen through the jammed blocks up which one climbs. Above this an excellent pitch of steep slabs is climbed up a groove on the left. Easy scrambling to a gap. Beyond rises a very steep wall with a vertical slit down the middle. This gives 40 feet of most interesting climbing up a stretch of piled blocks. The climb now degenerates and finishes at the grassy col leading over and down into Fan Corrie. (J. 8.118–120, 152–156; 23.47.)

BACHELORS' CHIMNEY   350 feet   DIFFICULT

First ascent: W. W. Naismith, A. M. Mackay, F. G. Squance and H. Raeburn   *March 31st 1902*

This climb—originally Bachelors' Buttress—lies wholly in what was known as Central Chimney.

A grassy scramble leads to the foot of the chimney which has three good pitches. The first is a jammed-block with a through-route. Next comes a difficult wall-pitch, climbed by a groove on the right. Finally a large upper chokestone is climbed by a cave pitch on the left. This leads to broken ground and a ledge. From this point much variation is possible. (J. 7.121, 178, 275.)

FAR SOUTH ROUTE   350 feet   DIFFICULT

First ascent: G. S. Ritchie and J. Pilnáček
October 5th 1947

The southern edge of No. 2 Buttress starts with a grassy rib of 200 feet overlooking 2/3 Gully.

Climb the rib until it abuts against the left edge of the main wall bounding Bachelors' Chimney on the left. From this junction a difficult open chimney leads to a ledge which traverses the wall without reaching Bachelors' Chimney. Move left and round the edge of this upper wall to reach easy ground. After 70 feet take to a ledge leading back to the right, then go up the face to a point above and left of exit of Bachelors' Chimney. Easy climbing to the top.

THE exact lines of the following climbs on the face between Bachelors' Chimney and Rose Ridge have not been traced. The accounts of their pioneers written in article form are very vague.

MARRIED MEN'S BUTTRESS   N.C.

W. W. King, A. E. Maylard and G. A. Solly
March 31st 1902

Prolonged investigation failed to trace this route. From the original description it must lie between Bachelors' Chimney and Rose Ridge, both of which are well defined. It seems unlikely to be the very steep rib immediately north of Bachelors' Chimney as suggested in C.G. 1950. This proved very hard on investigation and did not correspond to the description given. It probably lies between this rib and Rose Ridge. Here there is an ill-defined rib, mainly scrambling, giving access to the upper rocks above the level of the exit of Bachelors' Chimney. The initial rocks may have been snowed over on the first ascent and this may be responsible partly for the confusion. For original description see J. 7.121.

BELL'S ROUTE   N.C.

J. H. B. Bell, C. M. Allen and D. Myles   *May 14th 1932*

For original description see J. 20.10.

FAN CORRIE

The best and steepest of the upper corries. It funnels
into 2/3 Gully below and harbours two large buttresses
and many ribs.

Direct entry to the corrie is not altogether easy in
summer by way of 2/3 Gully—there are steep, waterworn slabs and it is not recommended. The easiest way
of approach is to climb the steep mixed rock and heather
slopes of No. 3 Buttress and traverse in above 2/3 Gully;
the best method is to ascend one of the routes on No. 2
Buttress to the grassy col and descend into the corrie.

Diamond Buttress, one of the best climbs on the face
is the right-most of the two large buttresses at the head
of the corrie. Its neighbour lacks its continuity and
provides steep scrambling only. (T. W. Patey and G.
McLeod, January 1956.)

In winter Fan Corrie carries steeper snow than the
other upper corries. The snow-rakes between the ribs
give good straightforward climbs to the summit ridge;
innumerable exits provide a wide choice as to difficulty.
A good, direct line starting in 2/3 Gully is up the rake
between Diamond Buttress and its neighbour to the
summit of Sgòran Dubh Mòr, the whole affording 1500
feet of easy but interesting climbing.

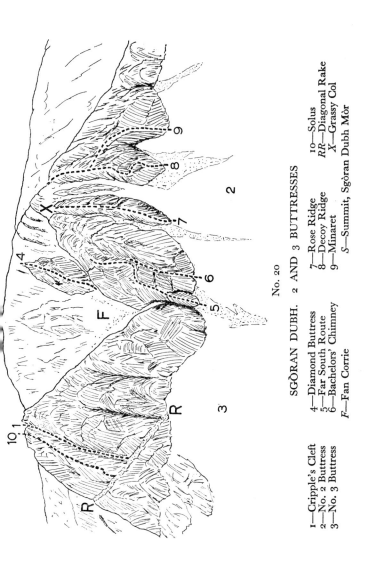

No. 20

SGÒRAN DUBH. 2 AND 3 BUTTRESSES

1—Cripple's Cleft
2—No. 2 Buttress
3—No. 3 Buttress

4—Diamond Buttress
5—Far South Route
6—Bachelors' Chimney
F—Fan Corrie

7—Rose Ridge
8—Decoy Ridge
9—Minaret

10—Solus
RR—Diagonal Rake
X—Grassy Col
S—Summit, Sgòran Dubh Mòr

DIAMOND BUTTRESS   400 feet   VERY DIFFICULT

First ascent: J. H. B. Bell, C. M. Allan and D. Myles
May 14th 1932

The upper and lower parts are in the form of a true ridge; a wall of rather severe angle forms the middle section. A good climb with one hard pitch.

The lower arête of 200 feet is fairly easy and leads to a broad ledge. The wall above is climbed just to the right of a fine tombstone belay—steep for 40 feet, then access to a hidden 15-foot chimney (V.D.) leading to satisfactory upper rocks and good belay. The upper arête has one or two gaps which are easily passed and the climb finishes on the upper slopes a short distance below the summit of Sgòran Dubh Mòr. (J. 20.11.)

Variation: The northern flank has been climbed. The first 80 feet or more is very steep, even sensational, with small, but good holds. Then easier ground to join the direct route. (J. H. B. Bell and Miss I. Bell, August 31st 1940. J. 23.47.)

THE most defined feature to the right of Diamond Buttress is Fan Rib. Between them are two smaller ribs, one above and to the right of the other. On them has been bestowed the names Nig and Nog.

NIG   150 feet   VERY DIFFICULT

First ascent: J. B. Hyne, F. L. Swinton and R. Harper
October 4th 1953

The southernmost of the pair—easily recognised by a block pinnacle at the top. Go up short walls and climb a crack of 40 feet. Move right and go up a steep corner for 50 feet then climb to left of summit block. An 8-foot drop to the neck. Go right to the start of Nog.

NOG   200 feet   DIFFICULT

First ascent: J. B. Hyne, F. L. Swinton and R. Harper
October 4th 1953

An easy rib to an awkward step right into a groove.
Climb the groove and the 50-foot wall above. Piled
blocks lead to the summit of a pinnacle and then there
is a short descent to a neck. A slab of 30 feet, then a
15-foot crack on small holds before stepping right to end
up ribs. Artificial but a good finish.

FAN RIB   250 feet   MODERATE

First ascent: J. F. Scott and K. McLaren
October 6th 1940

The climb starts steeply up cracked, rather holdless
slabs, then narrows to an arête of piled blocks. Two
thirds up, a short chimney may be avoided on the left by
stepping round an exposed corner to a platform, from
which a strenuous pull-up is made to easier rocks. The
angle eases and there is no further difficulty. (J. 22.320-1)

THE long subsidiary rib—part of No. 2 Buttress—to the
left of the upper part of Far South Route has been
climbed. The rib itself is nowhere more than a moderate
scramble but access to its start is more difficult—a wet
chimney on the right wall above the second pitch of
2/3 Gully. The upper part of the rib terminates to the
right of Fan Rib, but considerably lower.

No. 3 BUTTRESS

This takes the form of a steep wall rising above smooth
slabs on the left and heather slopes on the right. The
prominent (though at close quarters ill-defined) Diagonal

Rake runs upwards from right to left across the wall which is divided vertically by several chimneys. The buttress is not fully worked out.

ORIGINAL ROUTE   N.C.

First ascent: H. C. Boyd, S. A. Gillon, A. M. Mackay and
       H. Raeburn   *March 28th 1902*

The route is impossible to trace from the pioneers' description. It was probably on the left side of the buttress, but the possibility of the right side should not be discarded as snow covered the lower section. This may have misled them as to the extent of the slabs.

Their account (abridged) is as follows. "The lower slabs were snow-covered and readily passed. The edge of the buttress above was climbed without great difficulty for about one third of the height. A steep wall offering for hold only shaky flakes then compelled a traverse to the right. The ridge above was gained by a small snow-paved gully." (J. 7.120, 275.)

CRIPPLE'S CLEFT   300 feet   VERY DIFFICULT

First ascent: R. B. Frere and P. A. Densham
                        June 7th 1945

As viewed from the site of the Upper Bothy a thin crack with four or five chokestones in its lower part, cleaves the upper cliff commencing more than half-way up the Diagonal Rake. This is the climb. The approach by the Rake is treacherous, but variation may be possible.

Climb first pitch by wall on left. The second presents no great difficulty. The cleft steepens to present the hardest section where one tricky move is required (V.D.). Another chimney pitch and the cleft widens to an open gully in which there is no difficulty to the top. (J. 23.350.)

SOLUS   300 feet   DIFFICULT

First ascent: R. B. Frere   *Possibly 1952*

On the buttress or rib bounding Cripple's Cleft on the left.

The base is steep and slabby so move left into a gully. Climb this for 40 feet on somewhat shaky holds then traverse right on to the buttress which continues to rise steeply for about 200 feet but is well furnished with holds and only moderately difficult. Near the top climb an obvious, exposed 15-foot crack on the left to easy ground.

No. 4 BUTTRESS

This presents a considerable frontage to the loch, but is rather broken up and carries much heather. The upper part of the buttress is quite an extraordinary piece of rock architecture—a profusion of fine towers cut by deep gullies—but not offering continuity of climbing.

Seen face-on, the most conspicuous feature of the mass is a deep-cut slabby gully set about the centre with the Tower on its right flank. The gully and both its flanks have been climbed, that on the right being selected on the first ascent of the buttress.

ORIGINAL ROUTE   450 feet   MODERATE

First ascent: A. M. Mackay and party   *June 21st 1902*

Easy heather-clad rock on the right flank of the gully to the Tower. The difficulties on this proving too great, the party turned it on the right and followed the second of several chimneys striking up to the ridge behind the Tower over two pitches each of 60 feet. (J.7.119, 178, 276.)

The Tower can be ascended directly—tackle it straight

ahead by a 30-foot vertical face which leads to a sloping ledge running parallel to the crest. When the ledge peters out, continue up a short vertical crack to the crest and over slabs to the top. The climb is exposed throughout. (R. B. Frere and party, September 9th 1950.)

ALSO on No. 4 Buttress but at right angles to the frontal face and hidden from the usual approaches is a fine array of miniature ridges flanking Coire na Cailleach under Sgòr Gaoith and facing No. 5 Buttress. Although impressive they are unlikely to hold much technical interest. Higher up, however, three distinctive ribs taper and converge towards each other and exit directly on to the summit ridge. They face out across the glen and are bounded by the tiny tributaries of the burn on the immediate left of No. 4 Buttress. The central and most attractive has been climbed:

EINICH RIB   300 feet   DIFFICULT

First ascent: J. Bruce, A. Brebner and G. McPherson
April 19th 1953

Presents a broad front. Start at the centre up a little semi-detached arête then go straight up the face for 200 feet on very steep rock but well furnished with holds. A short, easy upper arête follows.

No. 5 BUTTRESS OR PINNACLE RIDGE

The last buttress in the line, characterised by a striking obelisk or pinnacle above mid-height (A' Chailleach— The Old Woman). The buttress looks particularly impressive from Coire Odhar at the head of the loch, from which position the Pinnacle stands out prominently.

A deep gully well seen while ascending the glen cleaves

the right-hand wall of the buttress—No. 5 Buttress Gully.
This should not be mistaken for the Slash, an impressive,
unclimbed gully-chimney further left, which is by far
the most conspicuous when the buttress is viewed directly
across the loch from its eastern shore.

The actual right-hand edge of the buttress gives easy
climbing as far as the Pinnacle, but as one passes left
towards the Slash unbroken slabs take the place of
heather ledges. Beyond the Slash heather takes over
once more.

PINNACLE RIDGE   1200 feet   MODERATE

First ascent: H. G. S. Lawson and H. Raeburn
March 8th 1902

Follow the right-hand edge without difficulty as far as
the Pinnacle. There are three routes to its top:

(*a*) Traverse the north side to reach the neck behind,
whence there is a fine 30-foot knife-edge leading back to
the summit (the pioneers. Difficult).

(*b*) Start directly from the lower edge. Just before the
top one is forced to make an exposed traverse on the
north face. (J. H. B. Bell, March 1935. Difficult.)

(*c*) By the north arête (W. T. Hendry, July 1943.
Difficult).

Above the neck there is more steep scrambling to a
small tower and col marking the top of No. 5 Buttress
Gully. The steep rocks of the final tower bounded on
the left by a deep gully follow immediately and then the
climb degenerates to an easy ridge running up to the
summit of Sgòr Gaoith. (J. 757–60.)

Winter: No records. This would provide a fine, long
route—Alpine in character after heavy snow, though
probably not very hard.

No. 5 BUTTRESS GULLY   600 feet   VERY DIFFICULT
GRADE 2

First ascent: G. R. Symmers and Miss N. Bruce
July 8th 1929
First winter ascent: T. W. Patey and A. Beanland: L. S. Lovat, J. Y. L. Hay and Miss E. M. Davidson
January 2nd 1956

Two tiers of chokestones are jammed in the narrow inlet of the gully. The first pitch is short and not difficult. The second if taken direct involves a strenuous pull out of a little cave. The gully now becomes slabby and slimy. The easier alternative is to climb the buttress of mixed grass and rock on the right. (C.C.J. 12.48.)

Winter: During severe weather all pitches may be obliterated bar the second which, however, provides the only real difficulty under snow. The first and second pitches were not banked on the first ascent and carried some ice. Higher up there were several minor pitches— easy on good hard snow. As time was short the party traversed left above the col and climbed the deeply-cut gully which led to the easy upper ridge. $1\frac{3}{4}$ hours.

SOUTH of the buttresses and between them and the horseshoe of Coire Odhar is the corrie known as A' Phòcaid—The Pocket. Here there are good gullies in winter striking up behind No. 5 Buttress, but no summer work.

MARGINALIA

COIRE GARBHLACH OF GLEN FESHIE

This unique corrie is of interest more for its singular beauty than for its rock-climbing potentialities. It is a narrow, trenched valley rather than cirque, with steep walls composed in the main of grass rakes with vegetated, fragmentary buttresses. The predominant rock is schist though gneiss is present also. In summer there is one recorded route. In winter there should be fair climbing giving sporting routes to the summits which share the corrie, Meall Dubhag and Mullach Clach a' Bhlàir.

APPROACH

From Kincraig by driving roads on either side of the Feshie. That on the east to Achlean is suitable for light cars; that on the west may have a locked gate at Tolvah.

HERMIT'S RIDGE   350 feet   VERY DIFFICULT

First ascent: D. Myles and J. H. B. Bell   *October 5th 1932*

The lower corrie bends and narrows before opening out into the upper. There is a waterfall at the junction. High up on the left of the waterfall is the longest stretch of rock in the corrie. Here is the Ridge. To its right a steep recess rises to a prominent cave.

The lower difficulties on the ridge can be avoided. About half-way up a small tower can be climbed direct or turned on the left. Beyond a small col a vertical 60-foot wall blocks the way. Climb this direct on good holds (test carefully, M.S.) or alternatively make a short descent to the right giving access to a 60-foot chimney leading back to the crest (V.D.). Easier climbing to the top. (J. 20.70.)

THE faces of Coire Mharconaich and Creag Mhigeachaid are devoid of climbing interest.

STRATH NETHY

The main features here are Coire Dheirg of Bynack More and the cliffs of the Sròn a' Cha-no the north top of Cairngorm.

Coire Dheirg containing the reddest screes in the Cairngorms is a beautiful and colourful miniature corrie, but its buttresses, which have been explored (earliest record A. M. Mackay and party, June 1902), are short (*c.* 250 feet) and indefinite. The corrie, however, gives good though easy snow climbing, the best line being a Y gully centrally placed between the buttresses.

The easterly side of Cairngorm rises very steeply from the Garbh Allt in many places in belts of disconnected slab and the only defined rock lies on a crescent of granite high up under the plateau of Sròn a' Cha-no. The rock is good but the climbs are of no great length.

The rocks of Stac na h-Iolaire on Mam Suim are worthless from a climbing point of view.

THE TORS OF BEN AVON AND BYNACK MORE

These unusual features give interest to what are (from the climbers' point of view) otherwise dull mountains.

Ben Avon is liberally sprinkled with them and the top of one is in actual fact the highest point of the mountain and requires, ironically, the use of hands to get there. The most interesting of Ben Avon's tors for the climber is the Clach Bun Ruadhtair on the west side of the Caol Ghleann about half a mile west-north-west from Coire Lochan nan Gabhar. There are three immense masses of granite of which the centre is the highest (80 feet). For details see J. 23.355.

On Bynack More the tors are known as the Barns of Bynack. They lie half a mile to the south-east of the summit and all have been climbed. For details see J. 23.350 and C.C.J. 10.241.

ADDENDA

The information on the following routes has arrived too late for their lines to be shown on the diagrams:

Hell's Lum Crag

BRIMSTONE GROOVE 250 feet MILD SEVERE

First ascent: G. Annand, R. H. Sellers and R. Reid
October 1958

Prominent break in upper cliff between Deep-Cut Chimney and Hellfire Corner. Lower part is not defined and start is over slabs.

Follow slanting fault leading to Deep-Cut and start on glacis immediately below Groove. Go up a slab rib on small holds just beneath a projecting nose for 30 feet. Traverse right till under small "dièdre". Use piton high up and a sling to reach hold on right edge, then swing to right wall. Go straight up wall to ledge. Surmount nose above by cracks, then go up fault, now at easy angle and on good holds until it steepens again beneath another crack (piton belay). Jam up crack and ascend steps to ledge in 100 feet, then to the top by two, large, moderate steps in 60 feet.

The Stag Rocks

DECEPTION INLET 450 feet SEVERE (V.)

First ascent: A. Thom, M. Smith and G. Annand
May 1960

The lower of twin grooves at the foot of Diagonal

Gully, demarcating buttress of Pine Tree Route. Steeper and more difficult than its appearance would suggest.

Go up a groove on left of small rock-mass at foot of Inlet then easily up grass into main groove. The next 100 feet provides a continuous pitch of sustained difficulty, very strenuous for the last 50 feet, particularly so in the final 15-foot overhanging groove. Piton belay at top. The groove widens to an amphitheatre. Go straight ahead over ledges and blocks to a wall in 100 feet. Climb a right-angled corner in the wall (30 feet, V.D.) and continue up steep but ledged rock then veer left up a wide depression to a short arête leading to top.

Coire an t-Sneachda

SPIRAL GULLY	350 feet	GRADE 2

First ascent (winter): T. W. Patey   *February 1959*

The gully immediately to the right of Crotched Gully, biting deep into the columnar upper crags bordering Fingers Ridge as it spirals to the right. No real pitches under heavy snow conditions, but steep and interesting. Not a summer climb.

THE MESS OF POTTAGE: This is the ill-defined crag left of Jacob's Ladder. In summer it may not offer worth-while climbing. In winter two routes have been worked out.
1. On the broken right flank is an obvious snow route offering several lines.
2. A steep, diagonal staircase climbs leftwards in the middle of the crag. This is severe on iced rock. The direct finish was not completed; a 10-foot traverse to the left was the escape.

J. H. Deacon and T. W. Patey. February 1960

Coire an Lochain

THE MILKY WAY   300 feet   GRADE 3

First ascent: T. W. Patey, V. N. Stevenson and I. W.
    Armitage   *11th February 1959*

The ill-defined gully 30 yards right of the Vent.
Although its ascent may have been made in summer it
is essentially a winter route.

The first pitch above a steep snow tongue, is a vertical
100-foot chute. On the first ascent this was avoided by
a 50-foot deviation to the top of the spur on the right
whence by a 120-foot lead on steep, mixed ground, the
gully was regained above the chute. The gully continues straightforwardly, finishing by a spiral trough
within the upper amphitheatre of the Vent. Time:
2 hours.

Garbh Choire Mòr

TIARA   300 feet   VERY SEVERE (V.)

First ascent: A. Thom, G. Annand and R. Wiseman
                                        June 1959

Follows the right edge of the buttress topped by impressive overhangs immediately left of Bunting's Gully.
The final traverse and crack are exposed.

Easy rock and vegetation lead to the start of the climb
150 feet from the screes. A moderate pitch leads to a
steep 40-foot wall overlooking Bunting's Gully. Climb
the wall by a stiff upward traverse to the left and enter
a long groove at the top. Follow the groove on the left
side of an arête to a stance behind a small pinnacle at
the apex of the arête which here buts against a steep
wall. Climb a strenuous 25-foot chimney (S.) on the

left then continue up the recessed section of slabs (S.) between the overhangs on the left and the unclimbed chimney of Bunting's Gully on the right to a stance 80 feet below the plateau (piton belay). From this point make a descending traverse to the left, go round a corner on to the face of the overhangs and almost immediately enter a 50-foot crack interrupted by three undercut blocks. These necessitate hard moves, the last V.S. Easier rock leads to the plateau.

Sgòr Gaoith: No. 5 (Pinnacle) Buttress

THE SLASH   800 feet   VERY SEVERE

First ascent: T. W. Patey and V. N. Stevenson
15th February 1959

The prominent gash in the lower slabs of the buttress well to the left of No. 5 Buttress Gully and marked by a tree at its entrance. Usually very wet. First ascent using crampons in semi-winter conditions with much ice-glazing.

1. A traverse up from right for 60 feet to gain gully bed and block belay above first pitch.
2. Direct ascent, which is dirty and vertical, avoided by climbing right wall for 50 feet up an inset corner to chokestone from which gully bed is gained by rappel.
3. Easy ground to next pitch.
4. The key pitch. A horizontal traverse on thin ice led back into the corner of gully (now a rounded groove). This was climbed direct, then for 80 feet with difficulty increasing, ascent was by wedging and using wet ice-nicks (100 feet).
5. A cave pitch of 60 feet surmounted by backing-up round the chokestone.
6. Easy snow for 150 feet.

7. Vertical corner-chimney, icicle-festooned and dripping wet (100 feet).
8. Easy snow to end of lower section at 500 feet.

The logical continuation was by the upper gully immediately above and ending in a deep cleft giving access to the crest of No. 5 Buttress near its top.

———————————

As new ascents are made the accounts are given in the Scottish Mountaineering Club Journal, published in the spring of each year. The Journal can be ordered through any bookseller. Accounts of new ascents should be sent to the Editor, S.M.C. Journal whose address can be found in the current Journal issue.

INDEX TO THE CLIMBS

No graded list of climbs is given in this Guide. In an area such as the Cairngorms, where routes lie on faces belonging to separate mountains or corries, it would be difficult to ensure that such a list was truly objective.

CAIRNGORMS

THE CORRIES OF BEINN A' BHÙIRD

	Class Summer	Winter	Diagram page	Text page
COIRE NA CICHE				
Carpet, The	VS	—	7	9
Grey Tower	S	—	7	14
Grey Tower, Chimney Route	S	—	7	14
Hourglass Buttress	VS	—	7	10
Jason's Chimney	S	—	7	12
Little Tower Gully	—	2	7	13
Quartzvein Route	VD	3	—	15
Sandy Crack	VD	—	7	13
Sickle	VD	4	7	11
Slugain Buttress	D	3	7	9
South Gully	—	1	7	13
Trident	S	—	7	8
Twisting Gully	M	2	7	10
COIRE AN DUBH LOCHAIN				
A Gully	—	1	17	18
B Gully	—	1	17	18
Birthday Route	MS	—	17	22
Bloodhound Buttress	NC	—	17	18
Crow-Step Route	VD	—	17	21
Main Rake	—	1	17	19
May Day Route	D	—	17	20
Polypody Groove	MS	—	17	20
Tantalus Gully	S	3	17	19
Winter Rib	—	2	17	18

225

COIRE SPUTAN DEARG OF BEN MACDHUI (*cont.*)

THE CRAGS OF COIRE ETCHACHAN
AND LOCH ETCHACHAN

THE LOCH AVON HORSESHOE

	Class Summer	Winter	Diagram page	Text page
CAIRN ETCHACHAN				
Battlements, The	M	—	90	88
Boa	S	—	90	85
Castle Gully	VD	—	90	93
Crevasse Route	MS	—	90	84
Eastern Approach Route	D	—	90	89
Equinox	VS	—	90	85
False Scorpion	VD	—	90	93
Guillotine, The	VD	—	90	86
Nom-de-Plume	VS	—	90	87
Pagan Slit	HS	—	90	88
Python	VS	—	90	86
Route Major	—	4	90	89
Scorpion	VD	5	90	92
SHELTER STONE CRAG				
Castlegates Gully	E	1	90	94
Castle Wall	D	—	90	96
Citadel, The	VS	—	90	98
Clach Dhian Chimney	VD	—	90	101
Forefinger Pinnacle, Routes on	See text		90	102
Pinnacle Gully	E	1	90	102
Postern	HS	—	90	99
Raeburn's Buttress	S	—	90	96
Sticil Face	HS	5	90	97
HELL'S LUM CRAG				
Deep-Cut Chimney	VD	4	105	106
Devil's Delight	HS	—	105	108
Escalator, The	M	3	105	110
Hellfire Corner	S	—	105	107
Hell's Lum	NC	2–3	105	104
Kiwi Slabs	VD	4	105	109
Pothole, The	VD	—	—	106
STAG ROCKS: STAC AN FHÀRAIDH: STACAN DUBHA				
Afterthought Arête	M	—	112	111
Amphitheatre Gully	NC	—	112	115
Final Selection	D	—	112	114

	Class		Diagram	Text
	Summer	Winter	page	page

STAG ROCKS: STAC AN FHÀRAIDH: STACAN DUBHA (cont.)

Pine Tree Route	D	—	112	114
Quartz-diggers' Cave Route	VD	—	112	111
Rectangular Rib	D	—	—	117
Relay Climb, The	VS	—	112	115
Ribbon Ridge	M	—	—	117
Serrated Rib	M	—	112	113
Shuttle, The	VD	—	—	118
Tenements, The	VD	—	112	116
Triple Towers	M	—	112	113

THE NORTHERN CORRIES OF CAIRNGORM AND BRAERIACH

CAIRNGORM: COIRE AN T-SNEACHDA

Aladdin Buttress				
Direct Finish	S	—	121	124
Lamp Direct, The	S	—	121	124
Original Route	VD	4	121	123
Aladdin's Couloir	—	1	121	122
Aladdin's Mirror	—	1	121	125
Central Gully	—	1	121	126
Crotched Gully	—	1	121	126
Fiacaill Buttress	D	—	—	128
Fiacaill Couloir	—	3	—	128
Fiacaill Ridge	E	—	—	129
Fingers Ridge	D	—	121	127
Jacob's Ladder	—	1	121	122
Pygmy Ridge	M	—	121	125
Red Gully	—	2	121	127
Rib, The	D	—	—	123
Runnel, The	—	2	121	126
Western Rib	M	—	121	127

CAIRNGORM: COIRE AN LOCHAIN

Central Crack Route	M	3	130	133
Couloir, The	E	1	130	134
Ewen Buttress	M	3	130	134
No. 1 Buttress	NC	—	—	131
Savage Slit	VD	4	130	136

DEVIL'S POINT: BEINN BHROTAIN: CÀRN A' MHAIM

THE BUTTRESSES OF SGÒRAN DUBH MÒR AND SGÒR GAOITH

THE BUTTRESSES OF SGÒRAN DUBH
MÒR AND SGÒR GAOITH (cont.)

FIRST AID AND RESCUE POSTS

Stretchers and First Aid Equipment at the following Mountain Rescue Posts:

NORTHERN CAIRNGORMS

Loch Morlich Y.H. - - - -	Warden
Achnagoichan, Rothiemurchus (N.G.R. 914082)	- Mr McDonald
Gordonstown School - Alltyre House, Forres	- Mr J. M. Gillespie (Tel. Forres 2)

SOUTHERN CAIRNGORMS - - Derry Lodge

EASTERN CAIRNGORMS - Police Station, Braemar

Area Rescue Organisers

Application should be made via the Police to:

NORTHERN CAIRNGORMS	Mr John Aird, Planefields House, Inverness Tel. Day: Inverness 800 Night: Inverness 1158 Dr J. M. Brewster, Carrick, Forres Tel. Forres 207
SOUTH AND EAST CAIRNGORMS	Mr G. A. Roberts, 111 Great Southern Road, Aberdeen Tel. Aberdeen 24807